HUNTINGTON LIBRARY PUBLICATIONS

William A. Spalding

AUTOBIOGRAPHY OF A LOS ANGELES NEWSPAPERMAN 1874–1900

William Andrew Spalding

EDITED WITH AN INTRODUCTION
BY ROBERT V. HINE

Huntington Library, San Marino, California

Henry E. Huntington Library and Art Gallery
1151 Oxford Road, San Marino, California 91108
www.huntington.org

Book design by Ward Ritchie
Cover design by Doug Davis
Images from items in the Huntington's collections are reproduced by permission.

Front cover: Spring Street looking north from First Street, Los Angeles, c. 1885. C. C. Pierce collection, Huntington Library.

Library of Congress Cataloging-in-Publication Data
Spalding, William Andrew, 1852–1941.
  Autobiography of a Los Angeles newspaperman, 1874–1900 / by William Andrew Spalding ; edited with an introduction by Robert V. Hine.
     p. cm.
  Includes bibliographical references and index.
  ISBN 978-0-87328-229-1 (pbk. : alk. paper)
  1. Spalding, William Andrew, 1852–1941. 2. Journalists—United States—Biography. 3. Journalists—California—Los Angeles—Biography. I. Title.
  PN4874.S58A3 2007
  070.92—dc22
  [B]
                              2007002130

PREFACE

WILLIAM ANDREW SPALDING wrote his autobiography when he was nearing his eightieth birthday, still alert and vigorous. He called it "The Autobiography of an Ordinary Man," but the fact that he dictated over five hundred close-packed pages was one indication that the title was a misnomer. An even clearer sign was the substance of the work itself—the man's life. Each of the four main divisions of his life—divisions which are equally clear in the manuscript—shows the man to be unusual: the self-reliance of his early years in Ann Arbor, Michigan, 1852-1865; his rapid maturation during school days and adolescence in Kansas City, 1865-1874; the ability to sense opportunity during his Los Angeles newspaper career, 1874-1900; and the rugged independence of the period following retirement, 1900 to about 1930, when he wrote his memoirs.

Only the third of these sections is published here. In the first two parts Spalding relied on a remarkable memory, delighting to prove he could recall detail after detail of his childhood and youth. For the journalistic years he was able to refresh his mind substantially by thirteen scrapbooks of his own articles clipped from the papers. These scrapbooks are now in the Huntington Library, along with a collection of letters and miscellaneous writings—all of which have been used in the editing.

The original "Autobiography" was typed in two copies: one of these is now in the Huntington Library, the gift of Mrs. Mary Louise Spalding Cooper, a daughter, and the second in the possession of Mrs. Helen Spalding Groff, the other surviving daughter. Until he died in 1941 Spalding penciled additions or corrections sometimes on one copy and sometimes on the other. Both versions have been at hand in editing the present work, and editorial discretion has determined which of the changes to follow.

Spalding's paragraphing has at times been revised. A few misspellings have been corrected, but foreign phrases and the hyphenation of words have not been altered. Some punctuation has been edited (simplified, for example, in the many instances that commas and dashes were used together, and changed occasionally for clarity). Newspaper titles have been italicized whether Spalding did so or not. Deletions have all been indicated either by bracketed comments or by footnotes. Otherwise the "Autobiography" as here reproduced stands as Spalding wrote it.

Mrs. Helen Spalding Groff has from the beginning provided inspiration and invaluable assistance. Dr. John E. Pomfret of the Huntington Library initiated the work by early recognizing the historical importance of the manuscript. In the editing process Dr. Edwin H. Carpenter of the Huntington Library, Dr. Doyce B. Nunis of the University of California at Los Angeles, and Dr. Edwin R. Bingham of the University of Oregon have been particularly helpful. To the Automobile Club of Southern California are due special thanks for preparation of the map of Los Angeles. To the Board of Trustees of the Huntington Library for making publication possible and to the staffs of the Huntington Library, the Los Angeles Public Library, and the library of the Los Angeles County Museum go my sincerest thanks. But no one has worked as hard or as effectively on this edition as Miss Mary Jane Bragg of the editorial staff of the Huntington. Without her, many more errors would have crept in and much that is desirable would be missing.

R. V. H.

Riverside, California
September 1, 1960

CONTENTS

ILLUSTRATIONS

INTRODUCTION

CHANGES IN AMERICAN JOURNALISM during the last quarter of the nineteenth century were nothing short of revolutionary. Frank Luther Mott calls the New Journalism "a great turgid flood" and dates it from the year a lanky, Goyaesque immigrant by the name of Joseph Pulitzer bought the St. Louis *Post-Dispatch*, 1878. Editors catered to a wider public, including workingmen and women, circulation skyrocketed, and as a result another form of big business emerged; these were elements of the revolution.

The year Pulitzer purchased the *Post-Dispatch* a young man of twenty-six, William Andrew Spalding, had been reporting for newspapers in Los Angeles a scant five years. He was learning the trade, and from the bottom up. His hiring seemed straight from Horatio Alger. The editor said in effect—and we can almost see him scowling from beneath a green visor—if you want a job, go out and get me a story. Knowing little of news reporting, Spalding walked the dusty, sleepy main street of Los Angeles and, standing discouraged in front of the Pico House, saw weeds growing in the park. He wrote an editorial on the shame of a dilapidated Plaza; he passed the test and was hired.

Spalding's work with Los Angeles newspapers fell into three periods, separated by two interludes. The first seven years from 1874 to 1881 were with the *Herald* and the *Express* in almost every position from reporter to city editor. Then followed an interruption of four years in which he tried farming but was gradually eased back toward the blue pencil. Near the end of this interval he edited successively, though briefly, the *Rural Californian* and the Riverside *Press and Horticulturist*. The second important period, however, was with the Los Angeles *Times*, from 1885 to 1893. These were vital, formative years for that journal's editor, Harrison Gray Otis, the champion of conservatism, the bête noire of organized labor, and Spalding helped the *Times* through its initial great fight, the "big strike" of 1890. In the succeeding interim he served on the first state building and loan commission. And then came his third and finest newspaper hour from 1897 to 1900 editing, managing, and nursing back to health his first love, the Los Angeles *Herald*.

The roots of Spalding's career were planted in Ann Arbor, Michigan, where he was born on October 3, 1852, the youngest of four children. In analyzing his genealogy he was impressed with the fact that the old Saxon Spalding clans "were known as fighters" and that "as a race, the Spalding family has always been possessed of great physical vigor." He listed among his ancestors that Henry Spalding who took the word of God to the Oregon country in the 1850's, probably not because he was a missionary but because he was hardy. William's father, Ephraim Spalding, "after the manner of a long line of pioneers," drifted west from a New York farm to Ann Arbor, then still a frontier town. Among other things, Ephraim gave to his son canniness and doggedness, well illustrated on the occasion of a barn raising when Ephraim was faced with a difficult dilemma. Whisky was expected by his neighbors, and he did not wish to be considered stingy; but he did not believe in drink. He therefore bought a generous jug and standing before his assembled worker-guests poured the contents into the earth. In Ann Arbor, Ephraim was successively shoemaker, hatmaker, county sheriff (though he believed all men to be essentially good), and finally a prosperous hardware merchant. Much later William remembered how he, as a boy in his father's store, would "monkey with the solder and the soldering irons."

The Ann Arbor home was really a farm within the city, and he grew up, reserved and introspective, among peach and apple orchards, pigs, and cows. Willie recalled the house as a station of the Underground Railroad. His parents' free-soil sentiments were also embodied in a Republican flag, stitched with the likeness of Frémont, which was raised beside the house in 1856.

His mother was a Scotch Methodist who could quote Benjamin Franklin and the Bible without end, but she went to her church unaccompanied by husband or children. She tried to interest young William in the Bible, and he dutifully read to the third chapter of Genesis but as an old man admitted that "the remainder of the task is still hanging fire." He did read, however, probably because of its harrowing descriptions, Foxe's *Book of Martyrs*, one of the few books in the home.

The family moved to Kansas City in the spring of 1865, and there his older brother James, who had been graduated two years before from the University of Michigan, founded Spalding's Commercial College. Even using some of the father's capital, the school opened in a third-story loft, with only a dozen scholars. Young Willie, then thirteen, was one of the twelve, and at his brother's school he learned the mysteries of accounting and double-entry bookkeeping.

Once his brother by chance took him into Payne's Job Printing office, and the visit deeply impressed the boy. The type cases, the silent compositors, the clanking presses, "the very atmosphere of the shop—the smell of printer's ink, the self-centered quiet activity of the men—cast a spell over me." The spell was enhanced (or perhaps weakened) when he got a job at $15.00 a week as mailing clerk for the Kansas City *Journal*. There he slept in the rear of the composing room since his hours began at three in the morning. But he was soon doing more than mailing—bringing up the job printing stock, measuring the printers' "strings" by which their day's work and wages were determined, and by the time he was sixteen managing the books for the company, if only on a temporary basis.

With his savings he attended for a few months the University of Michigan, but financial stringencies developed for his parents, and he was forced once again to leave Ann Arbor. Back in Kansas City these were hard years. Spalding suffered malaria, worked intermittently as bookkeeper at a dry-goods store and a flour mill, and finally felt the depression of 1873 which knocked Kansas City hard. His closest friend, Fred Wood, took off for the Pacific Coast, and Spalding, who already had read Charles Nordhoff's gilded description of California, in a desperate gamble borrowed money and followed Wood west.

It was strange that a man should have seen Los Angeles in 1874 as more promising than the other California cities he visited—Oakland, San Francisco, San Diego. Los Angeles was a mean, a dirty, and, as Spalding said, a dull town. But the year Spalding arrived the first horsecar was drawn down Main Street, and many another man saw enough future in that horsecar to stay around. Stephen M. White, Joseph Lynch, Edward T. Wright, John F. Godfrey—all came within a year, one way or another, of Spalding's arrival. It is interesting that Spalding's newspaper career approximated the span of the horsecar in Los Angeles; he and the horsecar retired about the same time. But the first rattling electric trolleys were no more dramatic a change than Spalding was to witness in Los Angeles newspapers.

His novitiate editorial on the weedy Plaza was symptomatic of the early newssheet, usually the voice of a strong editor, self-appointed guardian of the public rights and virtues. Spalding's first Los Angeles years trained him in assuming that role. An auctioneer stacks his wares on the sidewalk requiring ladies in long skirts to step into the unpaved street. Spalding the next day caustically prints a complete itemized inventory of the trespassing goods, and they are moved. The election-day closing law for saloons is being evaded, and Spalding writes the story of a man who, setting out for the polls, never arrives because he is so intrigued with the "iced tea" served through the rear doors of every bar. And so he worked through the years, exposing everything from improper street drainage to improper morals, from the intimidation of a harbor ballast carrier to general intimidation at the polls, from the pollution of water supplies to pollution in state politics.

But as time passed he felt the pulse of the press becoming weaker, at least in certain causes. On his withdrawal from the *Express* in 1881 he believed "the newspaper business has greatly deteriorated." By the 1890's he had become genuinely disturbed. The year he retired, 1900, he spoke of the modern newspaper as a great machine in which "individuality is ground to an impalpable powder." Editors like Horace Greeley, once colossi, Spalding continued, "are growing smaller by degrees and beautifully less."

Instead of a newspaper with such a personality behind its utterances, we have a great mystery, a great impersonality, with many pages filled to the brim with sensations and chaff. It is a newspaper designed to catch the eye of the thoughtless, to pique the curiosity of the shallow, to amuse, to sell. It is taken very much as the dime museum is taken, and it exercises about as much influence on the serious thought of the age. It serves to pass an idle hour, and is thrown aside without leaving a single lasting impression on the mind of the reader.

What Spalding saw resulting from the increasingly corporate interests of the press—the growth of great chains, the purchase of papers by businessmen whose interests dictated policy—was not unique with Los Angeles. The newspapers of this area, however, though they were reflecting national trends, were at the same time playing a role unlike those of many other cities. Spalding's first paper, the *Herald*, for example, was in the 1870's not so much a reformer as a booster or, as it was once described, "the original journalistic boomer of Southern California." In such a niche Spalding's rural and suburban rambles fitted neatly.

James J. Ayers, Spalding's friend, once wrote, "it is universally conceded that Los Angeles has been more judiciously and attractively written up than any other portion of the United States." If not judicious, the accounts were at least attractive in a flamboyant way. They were premonitions of the first motto of the *Times*, "Push things!" And in the 1870's numerous communities arose to be pushed—Pomona, Spadra, the San Fernando valley,

Santa Monica, Colton. Spalding fanned flames which attracted many a moth.

Nor was he himself above attraction. The "Autobiography" is full of his side investments in land, and he later wrote, "if one has an urge for gambling, why poker or faro? What's the matter with playing one end against the middle in a small town that is destined to attain a million population? The player has to sit in longer, it is true, but think of the odds!"

These successful investments were one reason Spalding could leave the newspaper world. He could now afford to retire. The boosting of California had aided him directly. He had made magnificent mistakes, he had taken sickening losses through the years, and as a good Scotsman he continued to worry about finances; but as a matter of fact by 1900 he had "sat in" long enough, and his investments were relatively secure.

His financial independence, however, does not explain the finis he wrote to his life as a newsman in 1900. When he resigned from the *Herald*, he was only forty-eight, his most vigorous years still ahead, and it was not like Spalding to stop the fight just because he could afford to. In the "Autobiography" he says he quit because of overwork and sorrow at the death of his son. He had imagined Hamilton taking a course similar to Harry Chandler's —from circulation (where the boy was already succeeding on a Los Angeles newspaper) to leading managerial and editorial positions. The loss of Hamilton, the end of that dream, was one of the crushing blows of Spalding's life. But there was at least one other reason for the resignation, perhaps equally compelling, to which he does not allude in his "Autobiography." In a farewell editorial he said he was retiring because, "I hold views concerning issues prominently before the country which the stockholders of the *Herald* regard as too extreme for even a Democratic paper to take."

Spalding's political views, which were thus to force his retirement, did not mature quickly. In his early newspaper stories there is scant reference to politics. Like the country at large, he was not moved to politics by the occurrences of the middle 1870's, especially in Los Angeles. But in the year 1879 two events seem to have crystallized his thoughts: the publication of Henry George's *Progress and Poverty* and the California Constitutional Convention. Both were reactions against the excesses of big business in the Gilded Age, and Spalding was interested in George and actively supported the new Constitution. A new liberalism was developing in the country, and Henry George, pointing an accusing finger at the monster of monopoly, was part of it as were the constitutional reformers, trying to pull the corporate fangs which had been used in the political field. By 1880 Spalding was a member of the Greenback-Labor Party, signing petitions "resisting this latest enemy of our country and of human freedom—the rising oligarchy of wealth."

Such a growing political orientation produced the most curious contradiction in Spalding's career—a man of his liberalism becoming so closely associated with the conservative Los Angeles *Times*. Until the end of his life he held stock in the *Times*, serving for many years as secretary of the corporation. He worked on the paper for eight years, mostly in responsible editorial positions. Yet he must have disagreed radically with the political views of Harrison Gray Otis. On the question of organized labor, the two men had grounds for agreement; Spalding felt that the monopoly of a union was as evil as the monopoly of capital. But in such matters as tariffs or protection of business from governmental regulation—here the Republicanism of the *Times* must have grated.

Of course, these dichotomies may not have been as clear to Spalding in the 1880's, his early *Times* years, as they were to become later. He was never antagonistic to business or industry as such. From the beginning he had encouraged industrial enterprises in the city, and his papers frankly supported their own commercial advertisers. The detailed preoccupation with George B. Davis' fruit-drying factory is a good example. "We gave him columns and columns," wrote Spalding with no asperity and no exaggeration. Furthermore, his closest friends, like Fred Wood and George Safford, had by the 1880's become closely identified with concentrations of capital.

But in spite of his friends, he was learning some vital political and economic lessons, and his interests in the orange industry had much to do with this education. Local citrus growers, like farmers everywhere, had become pawns of the distributors, and by 1891 the middlemen reached the point of accepting no fruit except on commission and on disastrous terms. In that year Spalding became vice-president of a new Orange Growers' Union, which valiantly battled the distributors for a few years and then in 1893 dissolved into a larger organization which in turn became the California Fruit Growers Exchange (better known as Sunkist). In this concrete way Spalding continued to carry the banners of Henry George.

In the middle or late 1890's, just as with the country itself,

Spalding developed even more liberal ideas. During this decade he came to believe in the free and unlimited coinage of silver, in the necessity of fighting monopoly even if it meant the abolition of the institution of the corporation, and in the public ownership of utilities. By this time he had left the *Times*, but his new situation from a political standpoint was not a great improvement. Although the owners of the *Herald* were his friends, they were using capital supplied by members of the private City Water Company. And here he was, the champion of public ownership of utilities, editing a paper which because of its connections could not be used to voice the ideas of its editor. In short, he had become a Progressive with tinges of Populism, lashing out at big business when the profession for which he worked had grown into one big business in the service of another. The revolution in American journalism had hit home; Spalding did not like it and resisted by resigning. He told an antitrust conference in Chicago the same year that an iron rule held for editors who did not wish to conform to the views of capitalist owners— they were at liberty to face the wolf at the door. "I have some personal knowledge of this discipline; I have faced it, and I have concluded that it is better to face the wolf."

It was a tragic denouement, especially since those against whom he rebelled included his closest friends. He always remained loyal to Fred Wood and George Safford and Frank Gibson as men, even nursing Wood on his deathbed and subsequently watching over his widow, but deeply and almost inexpressibly he felt betrayed. The Woods and the Saffords had become successful, as he had; they were in positions of influence, as he was. But to his mind they represented an abuse of power, an attempt to control the press, and he represented the free, crusading editor of the past. Like Joseph he had been sold into Egypt.

It is perhaps the key to Spalding's life that his early boosterism, his love for his city, changed into political reformism, which in turn grew beyond the acceptable limits of a more narrowly defined press.

Following his retirement he wrote sporadically for liberal journals like the *Forward Movement Herald*, but most of the time he spent in public service and in quietly following personal interests. He had already served on the board of the public library from 1893 to 1895. Now early in 1900 he was elected to the Board of Freeholders, with men like the socialist H. Gaylord Wilshire, the reformer John Randolph Haynes, and Harry Chandler of the *Times*. He acted as secretary for the Civil Service Commission from 1903 to 1911 and continued as a member from 1911 to 1913 and from 1921 to 1923; he then became vice-president of the commission from 1923 to 1924 and finally president until his term expired in 1925. And he served on the City Planning Commission from 1920 to 1921. He was one of the founders and a board member of both the Museum of Natural History and the Southern California Academy of Sciences. He promoted and presided over the Los Angeles County Pioneer Society, editing and publishing for them the *Historical Record and Souvenir* (Los Angeles, 1923). These same historical interests led to his three-volume *History and Reminiscences, Los Angeles City and County* (Los Angeles, 1931). His income was supplemented for a few months in 1902 by auditing the accounts of the California Construction Company, the corporation which was building breakwaters for Los Angeles harbor.

All the while he had created a haven for himself at his Gates Street house, a third-story attic retreat, looking out from the hillside through deodars and palms across the eastern portion of his city. He probed the world of science, developing theories of the spiral in nature and the actions of earthquakes, corresponding with men like Daniel Coit Gilman, George Ellery Hale, David Starr Jordan, and Ellsworth Huntington. He had long been interested in the occult, and with a clear rational bias he continued exploration into mesmerism, thought transference, and the gloomy spheres of the séance. Against the hill he built for himself a separate studio in the form of a Hopi dwelling where he worked on pieces of unhardened cement as an experimental medium in sculpture. Cabinetmaking, gardening, inventions—his hobbies were a multitude. Like the boy in his father's hardware store, he was tinkering with the solder.

And he continued to write poetry. From his teens he had been addicted to verse. He early loved Robert Burns and Sir Walter Scott, but his own composition began when he picked up his brother's edition of John G. Saxe and laughed through the puns and satires of that genial poet. Much of the influence would stay with him. Saxe spoke of

> Poems by youths, who, crossing Nature's will,
> Harangue the landscape they were born to till;

and Spalding would write,

> Then spare the Muse, ye senseless scribblers all,
> Who, by your vile abuses, cause her fall,
> Who seek to gain a kingdom not your own,
> And reign from Poesy's unspotted throne!

[xviii]

The first Spalding words ever to appear in a newspaper were verse, for in the 1860's he was sending to the Kansas City *Journal* such items as "When Grant's the Ruler of Our Land." Poetry was not an unusual concomitant of nineteenth-century journalism, and Spalding, as his "Autobiography" shows, took full advantage of versifying skills in filling (or padding) his columns. Later in his life he wrote more serious stanzas, especially on occasions of death in the family. The passing of his son, Hamilton, for whom he had such glowing hope, resulted in his finest poem, "O Azrael," which concluded:

> . . . Is there for him
> A place within the Aiden land? For him
> Doth kindly Nature have a care? Say'st thou
> That such a life is not bestowed in vain,
> And such a death is not the wage of sin?
>
> Then said the Angel, Death: Dismiss thy fears;
> He that doth note the sparrow's fall and holds,
> Within the hollow of His hand the fate
> Of all created things, is just and good.
> 'Tis not for man to fathom all His ways,
> But be Thou satisfied; the end is Peace.

Most of his poetry was comic or lyric, but there was an occasional political overtone. Edwin Markham's "Man with the Hoe" he called "a living presence and inspiration to me," and he felt that he and Markham had been working in the same cause all their lives. When in 1921 Spalding privately collected his verse into a little book, *Snatches of Song*, he sent a copy to Hamlin Garland, whom he had earlier met in connection with their joint spiritualist interests, and Garland returned his compliments on the book: "It is all so American in its sincerity of emotion."

In an omitted section of the "Autobiography" Spalding recalled his boyhood intention to become a poet, but, he wrote, "I found that poets were a morbid and unhappy set, and many of them died young. Why waste one's life in vague yearnings—in soaring for the infinite and diving for the unfathomable?"

So in his retirement, a savant-patriarch with a vast variety of interests, Spalding lived his last forty-one years, nearly as many as before leaving the press, and he died on September 7, 1941, at his Gates Street house surrounded with scientific relics, leaves of poetry, and volumes of his yellowing editorials.

William Andrew Spalding was what David Riesman would call an "inner-directed man," one who carried a gyroscope within himself for guide and stabilizer. No frivolous social pressures ever warped his determination. Aboard the emigrant train for California his plug hat became an object of joke and ridicule, and, although the gibes stung, he retained the hat the more doggedly. He disliked the idea of saloons, and in the face of financial stringency he preferred to keep one of his buildings empty rather than rent to a vender of rum. His shooting match with Joseph Lynch was the sole resort which his internal guide allowed him short of cowardice.

The same inner direction dictated his religious life. Though his mother had failed to bring him to Methodism, for awhile in Kansas City he had been a Congregationalist, but "as my ideas enlarged with education," he said, "my faith in miracles weakened." The Unitarian Church in Los Angeles was his only other venture in organized religion. As a member of this church he adopted for himself a creed which completely eschewed the supernatural and stated simply: "I believe that this is the first Unitarian church of Los Angeles." The myths of the past, including Christ's divine origin and all blind faith, were, he believed, gradually being dispersed by the age of reason. He says in the "Autobiography," "There is no beneficent Providence that looks after the welfare of sheep or men." Or again, "a man must rely on his own moral force for protection from the temptations of life." He was a lone man struggling against the evils which society and environment had caused. His religious and his political liberalism walked hand in hand.

Up to a point he had been willing to close his eyes to what he considered wrong, but by 1900 the compromises were over. The inner direction had finally led him away from the church, away from his friends, and away from the press. In the whir of his gyroscope could be seen something of the Michigan frontiersman, that tall, erect father, and even more of his Scottish mother. And the motion finally broke the spell of the print shop, which had fallen on a boy in Kansas City over a quarter of a century before. Faced with the revolution which Mr. Pulitzer had ushered in, the inner direction and changing political orientation of a man triumphed, and a strong journalistic voice, like Prometheus bound, grew silent.

WILLIAM ANDREW SPALDING

Chapter I

SEEKING A NEW FIELD (1874)

I WENT TO OMAHA and took the Union and Central Pacific for the transcontinental trip. Considering my limited resources, I engaged the cheapest transit offered, which was then called the emigrant train. It was the slowest on the road, with no guaranteed time for the trip, but with reasonable assurance that, if the passengers stood by patiently, they would get through in a week or ten days. We not only took our time for running, averaging ten to fifteen miles an hour at the best, but the train was sidetracked at stations to allow passengers and fast freights to pass. The cars were of the plainest and cheapest construction, with no sleeping accommodations, the seats upholstered in a rattan woven fabric, with underplaced springs. There was an ample coal-stove in one end of the car, which kept us comfortable, and on which the emigrants were allowed to make their coffee. Every passenger provided his own hamper, as there was no assurance of stopping at eating stations. The emigrants also provided their own bedding. There were no curtains to be drawn for the sake of privacy, and the passengers in a car were like a big family, bunking together, mostly with their clothes on. Fortunately our car was not crowded, so that each passenger could appropriate a double seat, and this is the way we managed things for sleeping: The cushions were removable and both were taken out of their frames, and placed lengthwise. This made a bunk of sufficient width (and hardness) and long enough so that a person could stretch out nearly his full length; by flexing the knees a little it served, and beat sitting up all hollow. A handbag or folded overcoat might serve for a pillow, and, with the blanket or quilt provided, and the stove chucked up through the night, the situation was by no means bad. My dear old Mother had provided me an ample hamper—not only the usual substantials of bread and butter (the latter in a jar, so that it could be spread fresh) and boiled ham and eggs, and a baked chicken, and a fine large cake and cookies, and a jar of pickles, another of jam, another of jelly, and so on with all the relishes and tasty things her fertile mind suggested, but she had also provided, in little receptacles, tea, coffee, salt, pepper and ground spices. Why she had included the last named delicacies I could not devise, at first, but I found a use for them as this narrative will disclose further on. All of the emigrants seemed to be pretty well fortified against famine, and, if anything ran out or went bad, the larder could be replenished at some stopping place, where boys, girls and women came alongside the train, offering for sale bread, sandwiches, cake, pie, milk and other fresh viands. At that time of the year, and those distant stations, there was no fruit to be offered.[1]

In our car the passengers were all men, and we escaped that most intolerable nuisance of miscellaneous traveling, crying babies. There were five or six American boys at our end of the car, and a set of eight or ten young Germans at the other. Somehow the two crowds did not mix, possibly because the Germans were immigrants, and had not yet acquired the English tongue. But we let each other respectfully alone, and got along comfortably. They talked German altogether between themselves, and in the evening they had their wine and schnapps, and became jovial, singing their native choruses, and furnishing entertainment for everybody.

I cannot recall the names of all the boys in our set, but there were the two Fletchers, Frank and Charlie. They were evidently of good family, genial and jolly, but Charlie, the younger, was a rattlebrain, and Frank had to hold him down every now and

[1]Five years later, in 1879, Robert Louis Stevenson also crossed the country on the same route by emigrant train and recounted his experiences in *Across the Plains* (London, 1892). Stevenson's trip was more Spartan than Spalding's. For a bed Spalding could place the seat cushions lengthwise; Stevenson had to rent boards for a mattress. Because the car was not crowded, Spalding claimed a double seat to himself; Stevenson, however, for sleeping, as well as washing and eating, had to resort to the "buddy" system.

then. Another member was a raw, green boy of about fourteen or fifteen, of the typical back-woods Missouri type. He was dressed in jeans, and his belongings indicated that his circumstances were pinched and barren. But, withal he was a good-natured boy and quite loquacious in his crude Missouri vernacular, and stood all sorts of joshing, and we all formed a liking for him. He said he was from Posey county, and when asked if it was Hoop-pole township, said no, and gave some other name, without catching on to the concealed joke.[2] That was sufficient warrant for us to dub him "Hoop-pole," and by that name he was addressed for the rest of the trip. And he took it like a good sport. We boys got so chummy after a while that we exchanged little delicacies at meal-time—a pickle, or a spoonful of jelly, or some other little tasty—but poor Hoop-pole had nothing to exchange. His hamper contained only some loaves of bread, and a great hunk of jerked beef. But such as he had he ate without grumbling or excuse, and made no bones of the matter. The rest of us, admiring his pluck, made it up between us that we would help him out a little. So we developed quite a hankering for jerked beef, not all at once, of course, but about every meal some one would look longingly at that chunk and ask for just a little piece to remind him of old times, and Hoop-pole would seem to be really complimented, and would proceed to slice off a generous chunk—oh, three or four times as much as the hankering one would accept— for he wanted only a little piece, to remind him, and so forth. But, in exchange for that delectable morsel, Hoop-pole had to accept a pretty good helping of the choicer varieties of food. The next meal some other boy went through the same formula, and always, when we made coffee, Hoop-pole was invited to stand in for good-fellowship, and so he was enjoying what to him must have been quite a feast. After it got well systematized we all enjoyed the joke.

I mentioned that the villagers gave us opportunities to lay in fresh supplies. Once, about mid-continent, there was an extra quantity of milk on hand, and an idea struck me of a way to make good use of it. Requisitioning a flask of whiskey that one of the boys carried in his kit, I brewed a milk punch, on the big car stove. And that is where my spices came in. But if my provident

<hr/>

[2]Hoop-pole, in addition to being a nickname for the state of Indiana, referred to a place where grow small hickory or white oak saplings suitable for hoops; hence by implication an individual from such an area was a rustic or bumpkin. In one of Spalding's poems ("Uncle Peter") he wrote: "There are headings and staves close at hand for the taking, and plenty of hickory hoop-poles a-soak."

Mother had known to what use they were destined, I fear she might have had grave apprehensions. However we had a hilarious time over the punch, and nobody drank to excess, and what would you? The boys all declared me an artist in mixing and said the flavor passed all reckoning. How had I done it?

One of the minor incidents of the trip and one that was a joke from start to finish was my plug hat. In my callow days in Kansas City I had been guilty of the unspeakable folly of buying it. I suppose it was dear to my heart, and when I started out into the great world, it had to be taken along. There was no bandbox to protect it, but a string through the band furnished a loop by which it dangled from the rack above my head. If ever a boy was heart-sick of his vanity and folly, I was that boy. But I stood all the good natured banter about it, and after a time it became not the standing but the hanging joke. Although I was tempted a thousand times to throw it out of the window and be done with it, I still did not relish the notion of surrendering to the jokers, and thought I should get off easier by facing the thing through, than by showing the white feather. But that certainly was a case where a thing of beauty was not a joy forever.[3]

When we were near the end of our journey we had some excitement. Of course it came suddenly and unexpectedly. It was dinner time, and I had spread out my hamper on the seat and was engaging in my frugal repast, when Charlie Fletcher (the rattlebrain) came rushing down the aisle, and ducked behind my section. Immediately following him came one of the big Germans, with a revolver in his hand, and he bent over and leveled the weapon at Charlie, who was crouching on the floor. Without thinking of what I was doing, I grabbed the weapon by its barrel and wrenched it from his hand. Clubbing it, with a full swing of the arm, I dealt the German a blow in the middle of the forehead. I swung my arm for another blow, but just in the act I went down, and the weapon was wrenched from my grasp. When I had recovered my equilibrium the German crowd

[3]In Los Angeles' centennial celebration (1876), Spalding marched in procession with his lodge. "On that auspicious occasion I turned out with the Odd Fellows, and wore that plug hat which had come across the continent, dangling by a string. After that I gave it away to a poor man with a large family, and vowed never to march again." William A. Spalding, *History and Reminiscences, Los Angeles City and County, California* (Los Angeles, 1931), I, 244.

A long story has here been deleted concerning a proud Englishman who would have nothing to do with the common herd of travelers. He fell in with card sharps, however, and was forced to leave the train without money, belongings, or even hat. Spalding finished with a moral: "Pride goeth before a fall and a haughty spirit before destruction."

were forcing their turbulent companion back to their end of the car. He was raving like a crazy man. I proceeded to gather up the badly demoralized fragments of my hamper, and when I next looked up, it was to note that our crowd had all deserted to the next car. There I was left to face the whole German crowd alone. Every two or three minutes the crazy man would try to break loose, with the evident purpose of coming down to eat me alive. When he started my way, however, I calmly stood up in the aisle and put my hand back to my hip pocket. Although the captured weapon had been taken from me, and I did not know who had it, I felt pretty sure that the crazy German did not have it, and I had a little pistol of my own in that same hip pocket. It was not much better than a toy, and discretion told me that it was just as well not to show it. But the knowledge of its possession was a mighty comfort, and its undiscovered potentiality seemed to have a restraining effect on my furious antagonist; at least he allowed himself to be pulled back in his seat a couple of times after he had made a start. As for myself, I did not dare to run; that crowd of Germans would have been upon me like ravening wolves before I could get out of the car. So I held the fort alone, and as soon as the crazy man concluded to be less crazy, I settled into my seat, and made a pass at finishing my meal.

Pretty soon, finding that there was no shooting or further disturbance, our crowd sifted back, and we had a chance to compare notes. I could not find what had started the racket. All Charlie Fletcher would say was that he had gone down to have a little chat with the German fellows, and try to get acquainted, and one of them had taken offense at something he said, and had drawn a gun on him and chased him down the aisle. I found that the captured weapon which had been wrenched from my hand (lacerating one of my fingers badly in the process) was in possession of Charlie Fletcher. Whether he was the one who snatched it from me or not I could not find. But I demanded the weapon as it was properly my trophy, and Charlie finally gave it up on condition that I give him my own toy-pistol. I not only wished possession of the captured gun, but I wished to make sure that the crazy German did not get it again. My blow on his forehead had been hard enough to bend the metal frame of the handle and split the wooden filling. The next morning that fellow's face was a sight—both eyes blacked and a lump on his forehead as big as a walnut. When everything was fairly quiet I happened to catch his eye, and motioned him to come down.

He came, and I told him quietly that I had taken his gun because he was in the act of shooting a friend of mine, and I proposed to keep it. He was rather surly, but attempted no bluster. And so matters stood. Our crowd slept on their arms, so to speak, for the remaining two nights on the train, because we were uncertain what sort of come-back the Germans might attempt; but there was no further trouble.

My friend Fred Wood met me at the Oakland mole, and took me to the home of his father and mother in Alameda.[4] They were living in a modest cottage, and having come a year or so before, the doctor had established sufficient practice to provide a frugal sustenance. Dr. Wood was a rather stocky man with strong character and mentality. Had he not been a rolling stone he might have gathered more moss. He practiced medicine in the Methodist Church, and outside of that had ideas of his own. Mother Wood was a little bird of a woman, always cheerful and vivacious and, it seemed to me, always chirping and hopping. Fred had matriculated in the University of California at Berkeley for a special course in pharmacy, and had been studying about six weeks. I judged that his father had influenced him in that direction as a starter for studying medicine. If so, it was of a piece with the doctor's rolling-stone ideas, for Fred was already well advanced in civil engineering, and had held the position of transitman on the Chicago and Northwestern survey.

My arrival was in the middle of the week, and Fred had to be in attendance at his class for a couple of days, so I saw him only mornings and evenings. But that gave me a chance for a good visit with Mother Wood, and to look about Alameda a bit, and get rested up from my trip. Saturday Fred and I made a journey to Bay Farm Island to visit Aunt Purse and Uncle Benedict. Aunt Purse was Mother Wood's sister, and it seemed to me that two sisters could hardly be more unlike. Aunt Purse was stout and radiantly good-humored and chatty. I had never seen her before, but she readily adopted me for one of her boys, and devoted herself to planning nice things for Fred and me. Aunt Purse had never had children of her own, and she was just child hungry. Uncle Benedict was one of the pioneers of the island, and had piled up a competence in growing early vegetables for the San Francisco market. He had now retired from active gardening

---

[4]Fred W. Wood (1853-1900) had been a close school friend of Spalding's in Kansas City. He had lost his engineering job in 1873 before preceding Spalding west. Later events in his life will frequently be related in Spalding's text. See also Spalding, *History*, II, 327-330.

and leased his land at a good rate to various operators. He was rather a taciturn man, with a shrewd face and positive ideas when he did express himself.

We staid over night, and Sunday morning Uncle Benedict took us out in his row-boat for a ride on the bay and a duck hunt. It was my first trip on salt water and my first duck hunt. There was only one shot-gun between us, so we took turns at it. Uncle Benedict tried first, but got nothing. Then Fred banged away at a flock that was too far off. Finally it was my turn. Gun in hand I sat in the stern of the boat all eyes for the upper air. There was quite a breeze by this time; the water was choppy, and the boat bobbed about unconscionably. After a long probation of bobbing and watching, there came a flock flying low, right over the boat. "Here's your chance, Billy! Now! Now!" my companions shouted. I braced myself in a half standing position in the wobbly boat, and let go one barrel at the flock in general, not attempting to take aim. Judge of my astonishment and delight when a duck fell upon the water dead. We had no trouble in securing it, and it was my trophy. Of course it was the merest stroke of good luck; no marksmanship whatever. It was my first and my only wild duck. The satisfaction and glory of that feat was sufficient for a lifetime. Maybe it meant more than a wild duck to me; maybe I was inclined to be superstitious and look for an omen; maybe I said to myself, "Well, at last luck has changed for me in this new country."

In my visit with Fred and his family I talked freely of my ideas of a location, and my plan for going South to grow up with the future metropolis on the highway of international commerce. But I said not a word about Fred going with me. I took it for granted that, having entered the University, he would wish to finish his course, and that his parents would strongly urge him to this. But that Sunday afternoon, following the duck hunt and one of Aunt Purse's bang-up country dinners, Fred and I went out for a ramble over the farm, and of course we canvassed my prospects, fore and aft. Finally Fred said, all of his own motion, "Billy, I'm going with you." We shook hands on the proposition, and performed a Comanche war dance. But that celebration did not satisfy, so we drove a stake in the ground, and each in turn fired the German's revolver, to mark the spot and consecrate the compact. That duck certainly gave up its life for a good cause. My luck was coming up. Fred's people accepted his change of plans with equanimity, and even complacency. I think Mother Wood was rather pleased with the idea of Fred and myself double-teaming to go forth and find our fortune. The doctor's fancy for shifting was appealed to, and I miss my guess if he hadn't a little secret hankering to go along. "If you boys get established in that country," he said, "you can make a lot of acquaintances, and go into politics, and get yourselves elected to office."

At the first sailing date, which was early the succeeding week, we took passage on the steamer *Orizaba*, Captain Johnson, booked for San Diego. My exchequer had been practically exhausted by the trip across. I had in my pocket about $25, which would have barely sufficed to get me to my proposed destination. But Fred had $150 of his savings left. So we pooled our resources, under the firm name of Spalding & Wood, and started forth to hang tow on the bushes of Southern California, and seek our fortunes. I had seen nothing of San Francisco, except the general view in crossing the bay, and the closer glimpse of the water front when we went aboard the ship. San Francisco was too big, too much of a jumble, for either Fred or myself. We had neither of us been used to a large city, and would have felt utterly lost in it. And mere curiosity for seeing places was not the dominant thought in our minds. We wanted to go to that little dot on the map, whose greatness was all in the future, where we could get an even break, and a chance in the development. After all, isn't that the real pioneering spirit?

It was the first ocean trip for both Fred and myself. Looking through the Golden Gate was our first glimpse of the great Pacific, our first of any ocean. Of course everything was new, strange and full of interest. Fortunately for me, I was not troubled with sea-sickness. I fairly delighted in the rise and fall and the swaying of the ship, and could sit for an hour on the prow where the motion was at its maximum. Perhaps my immunity from sea-sickness was attributable to my preliminary bout with the intermittent-remittent [fever] and the long dosing with quinine. But Fred, poor boy, was not thus favored. However, he was not very sick, and managed to keep on his feet most of the time. Occasionally he would absent himself without any excuse, and go below for purposes unexplained, but I graciously refrained from being inquisitive on the subject, and the thing was passed off with a sly smile between us. I knew, and Fred knew that I knew, but why mention a disagreeable subject? One of our fellow passengers was a New York boy named Andy Lawrence. He was a thorough little gentleman, but did not attempt any airs, and was jolly, and we three flowed together like drops of water. He was bound for San Diego also, and hadn't much money, and was going to hang tow on the bushes, and there was a fellow-feeling all along the line. No wonder we became chummy on short acquaintance. Travel to the South must have been lively, for the best accommodation we could get was a mattress and bedding spread upon the floor of the dining cabin. But after my experience on the emigrant sleeper, the cabin bed was a real luxury.

We landed in due time at San Diego, and were impressed with the beautiful bay and the town rising on the long slope from the water front. San Diego was a place of two or three thousand inhabitants, with a predominant American atmosphere, and evidences of recent growth. The Horton House had been newly completed, and was the most pretentious building in the town. It was a long, substantial two-story brick structure fronting on a barren square called the plaza. On the other three sides there were one and two-story frame buildings occupied by stores, boarding houses, and a sprinkling of ground-floor offices. Fred, Andy and I registered at the Horton House, "just to gain a status," we argued, but after partaking of dinner, we paid our bills and checked out. It was altogether too high-toned and aristocratic for our slender purses.[5]

Meanwhile we secured a cheap lodging on one side of the square, and prepared for light housekeeping. Our regimen comprehended a light breakfast and an evening meal of pick-ups from the grocery store and bakery, and for dinner we went to a restaurant which afforded a very fair meal for 25 cents. We were for husbanding our resources from the beginning, because we did not know how long we should have to make them reach. When we required a rallying center to make observations on the passing world, we felt at liberty to loaf in the lobby of the Horton House. Were we not recent guests? And who had a better right to be there? Andy was the guest of some former New York family to whom he had taken a letter of introduction. But he rallied with us in our humble apartment for general confabs, or loafed with us in the Horton House lobby, and we counted him as one of the family. Andy had brought along his good clothes, and letters to a number of the high-up military officers in San Diego, and every day or so he had to rig himself out and go and make a call— perhaps attend a swell dinner, or some such nonsense. And he hated the hollow sham, and reviled himself shamefully. "A

[5]The Horton House, a magnificent hostelry, was only four years old in 1874. It was demolished early in the twentieth century to make room for the U.S. Grant Hotel.

pauper like me," he would say, "hobnobbing with a lot of military swells!" Andy's family must have been of the old-line New York aristocracy, for the letters which he brought commanded the highest social courtesies. Unfortunately, not much of the family wealth (if any) had come down to Andy; and the social courtesies, while gratifying in a sense, did not point to any practical way of getting on a bread-and-butter basis. Still Andy felt in duty bound to present all of his letters, and he hoped rather dismally that something would turn up somewhere.

Meanwhile, we were moving out into the business community, feeling the pulse. Every time we made a purchase for our larder, or could find some reasonable excuse, we talked with shopkeepers or artisans or wayfarers on the state of business and the outlook. Generally it was unfavorable. The facts were that San Diego had enjoyed quite a boom on the prospect of Tom Scott's much vaunted trans-continental railway, which was to make that place its Pacific Coast terminus. New subdivisions had been laid off and sold, and new buildings erected in anticipation of the great development just ahead. But Tom Scott's scheme had gone down in the crash of '73, and San Diego had been left with the bag to hold. Everybody was feeling the reaction, and many could see no hope ahead.[6] It took only a day or two for us to find the true state of things, and to realize that a sinking town was no place for a couple of young adventurers with our limited capital. But the going away was not so easy. We would have to wait a whole week for the next Northbound steamer. We even canvassed the proposition of buying ponies, and making our way overland to Los Angeles; but it is well we dismissed that idea, for it would have involved great hardship for a couple of greenhorns. After satisfying ourselves that San Diego was no place for us, we had to settle down to a mere matter of killing time, and as Tennyson has observed,

> The waiting time, my brothers,
> Is the hardest time of all.[7]

[6]The Texas and Pacific Railroad, chartered by Congress in 1871, was a project of Col. Thomas A. Scott of the Pennsylvania Railroad. Surveys were made in 1872 and local franchise and land grants completed—all of which resulted in a sizable San Diego boom. Construction had already begun and Scott was in Europe raising necessary funds when the Panic of 1873 dried up financial sources. It was San Diego's "greatest disappointment." Within a few years the city's population dwindled by one half. William E. Smythe, *History of San Diego* (San Diego, 1907), pp. 354-360.

[7]Sarah Doudney, "The Hardest Time of All," *Psalms of Life* (London, 1871), pp. 91-92.

A paragraph has here been omitted relating, among other details, Spalding's first taste of olives.

It must have been in this waiting period, with Andy coming in every day to "chew the rag" and our own disgust about killing time, that we put up on one wall of the room our motto:

Moralizing and Swearing Barred.

But even watchful and impatient waiting must have an end, and on schedule time Fred and I took steamer for the North. Andy was not quite ready to accompany us, having a few more duty calls to make, but if nothing turned up of a substantial character, he would soon follow. Our ship anchored in the deep water off Timms's Point and Banning's little transfer steamer towing a barge came out to take our passengers and freight. Thus conveyed to the Wilmington wharf, we took the train for Los Angeles. That railway of 22 miles was the only steam line in Southern California.

We arrived in Los Angeles late Saturday afternoon near the close of March, 1874, and registered at the old U. S. Hotel. The next morning, in default of anything better to do, we concluded to attend church. We made inquiry of Bob Eckert, the clerk, as to the location of the Episcopal Church. "Pistible Church, Pistible Church," he said, with a shake of his head, "No, I don't know." He had probably never heard of such a church. But a little inquiry on the outside soon directed us to it. St. Athanasius Episcopal Church, on the corner of Temple and New High streets, was within rifle-shot of the U. S. Hotel. Sunday afternoon we cruised about the old town until the edge of our curiosity was somewhat dulled, and returned to the hotel to talk things over and concoct plans.

Monday morning, as soon as we thought offices would be open, we betook ourselves to a corner room of the old Temple Block, to present a letter to Judge Thompson, of the firm of Lindley & Thompson, which Dr. Wood had given us.[8] Judge Thompson and Dr. Wood were both former residents of Galesburg, Ill. The Judge received us cordially, and was glad to hear from his old friend. He would do anything he could for his old friend's son and his chum. What sort of work had we done, and what sort of an opening were we looking for? Fred explained his former employment, and I told the Judge I had had more experience in a newspaper office than anywhere else. The Judge promptly gave

[8]John S. Thompson was a leader of the People's Independent Party, had been formerly active in the Grange, and helped the liaison between farmers and workers in the incipient labor movement. He was soon to become a city councilman, 1876 to 1878. His law partner was Charles Lindley.

[13]

me a note of introduction to Theodore Glancey, editor of the *Herald*, and told me where to go to present it. The *Herald* office was easy to find, for it was opposite the southwestern corner of that same Temple Block. Mr. Glancey, it seemed, was another Galesburg man.[9] I did not find out until afterwards, but my application to the Judge was just at the right psychological moment. The Judge was legal adviser to and a member of a syndicate that had just bought the *Herald*, and it was probably on his motion that Mr. Glancey, his former towney, had been employed as editor. So Mr. Glancey received me in a very pleasant way, and inquired as to my newspaper experience. I told him frankly that it had all been in the business department of the Kansas City *Journal*, and I didn't know much about news gathering. He wanted a little time to think the matter over probably, and he said, "I'm rather busy now; suppose you go out on the street and see what you can run down."

I accepted the indefinite assignment with misgivings in my heart, but there was nothing else to do. Fred was waiting for me on the opposite side of the street, and I promptly joined him and explained my dilemma. He must have noticed my consternation, for he said, "Whatever you do, Billy, don't get nervous about it. Let's walk up street, and maybe we'll see something, or something may happen." There was nothing better that I could suggest, so we walked past Temple Block, and then up Main Street as far as the Pico House and the old plaza. But nothing happened, and there was nothing to stir up an idea. But when we were standing in front of the Pico House, and I was wondering where to go next, my eyes fell on the old plaza, which was in a state of demoralization, and I had a glimmer. "I've got it!" I said, "Let's go back."

So we retraced our steps to the *Herald* office, which took only a few moments, and Mr. Glancey looked a little surprised at my speedy return, and more so when I asked for a table at which to write. In a few moments I had indited a screed on that deplorable old plaza, and an urgent appeal to the city authorities for its rejuvenation. I handed my copy to Mr. Glancey, and watched him, oh, so intently while he read it. Once I thought the corners of his mouth went up, and that was hopeful; once they went down, and that was ominous. But he finally looked up and smiled, and said: "That's all right. Right across the street is the Court House, and there you get all the court news. In the other corner

[9]Theodore M. Glancey had come from Illinois by way of San Francisco.

of Temple Block is Judge Gray's office; that is the justice court. A little further down this street is the city hall, where you get council proceedings and police news, and down at the foot of Commercial Street is the depot, where you get railroad and shipping news." Then I knew I was hired. Later he informed me that my salary would be $12 a week. Of course Fred was in ecstasies when I went to the hotel and gave him the good news.[10]

For the sake of accuracy and the complete elucidation of this narrative, I have taken the pains to overhaul an old file of the paper, fifty-eight years agone, and here is a transcript of my first item for the Los Angeles press, as printed in the *Herald* for March 25th, 1874:

The Plaza.

If it be in order, we would call the attention of our City Fathers to the present dismantled condition of our plaza. Like Mark Twain's "Baalbec," it is a most magnificent ruin. The fence is down in some places, the ground is overgrown with rank weeds and the fountain is very nearly in that poetical state of dilapidation described by Hood:

> "The fountain was a-dry—neglect and time
> Had marred the work of artisan and mason,
> And efts and croaking frogs, begot of slime,
> Sprawled in the ruined basin."

This state of affairs may be very romantic and all that, but it does not conduce to the credit of a city visited annually by thousands of people from every part of the world.

Let us have a small appropriation to improve the plaza, and thus add to the good looks, health and happiness of Los Angeles.

[10]Spalding's niece, Mary J. Spalding, noted in 1946 (MS in possession of Mrs. Helen Groff) that her uncle before he died had told of his first Los Angeles employment in this way: "Col. Ayers [i.e., Glancey] looked him over, and then asked him why he thought he could be a reporter. Your father told him of his experience with the Kansas City *Journal*, and added that it was his ambition to become a newspaper man. 'Well,' Col. Ayers said, 'you go out about town, find something to write a story about and bring it back to me tomorrow and I'll tell you whether or not you can be a newspaper man.'

"Your father . . . went out into the sunshine and sat down on a bench in the Plaza facing the old church. On the other end of the bench was an elderly man, evidently a Mexican, who looked at your father and said, 'Well, son, I take it you are a tenderfoot. When did you get here? Where did you come from?' etc. etc. Your father was just as full of questions about California and the town of Los Angeles.

"Finally the old man moved on, and all at once your father realized that he had material for a story. He hurried back to his room and wrote his article. The next morning he took it, with fear and trembling, to Col. Ayers who read it through, sat back in his chair and then said, 'Young man, you told me you arrived in this town yesterday.' Your father said 'yes Sir, I did.' 'Well,' said the Col., 'I have lived here two years and I didn't know that much about the place. Where did you get your information?' Your father told him about the old Mexican. The Col. replied, 'Well, you have written a fine story. You are hired!' "

My contribution was not a local item in form, but rather an editorial paragraph. Mr. Glancey could see on sight that I was totally untrained in newsgathering, as I had told him; but he took it as an indication that I had a fair knowledge of English and spelling, had something of a natural "newspaper nose" for available material, and might be trained to reporting by a little patience. At any rate that impromptu squib secured my job.

But another triumph in journalism awaited me. Two days later [March 27, 1874] appeared this paragraph in the *Herald:*

Our plaza is to lose its fine negligé and romantic appearance. The City Fathers have decided to put the chain gang to work there and renovate the place. Good idea.

So, my first item had brought down its duck. My good luck was continuing.

Chapter II

NEWSPAPERING:
THE *HERALD* (1874-1877)

———————————

A FEW WORDS concerning the founding and early history of the *Herald* may be in order. C. A. Storke, a young lawyer of Santa Barbara, married into the wealthy More family of that place, and received by way of dower ten thousand dollars in cash. With a great idea in his head and this dower in pocket, he came to Los Angeles and established the *Herald*.[1] He purchased a complete newspaper and job-printing outfit, and installed it in a good-sized ground-floor room of a single-story brick block on Spring Street, nearly opposite the old Court House. A part of the equipment was an upright boiler and engine of about five or six horse-power. This made it the only printing plant in Los Angeles operated by steam power. The first issue of the daily edition appeared Oct. 3d, 1873. There was also a weekly edition. The paper was avowedly Democratic, which showed a natural leaning, as there was no other organized party in Los

[1]Charles Albert Storke was a graduate of Cornell in 1870. He worked on newspapers in Detroit and Toledo before coming to California as an instructor at Santa Barbara College, 1872-1873. In the latter year he married Martha More, daughter of T. Wallace More, who gave Storke $4,500 for his Los Angeles journalistic venture. It is probably this amount that Spalding has misconstrued as a dowry. After his Los Angeles *Herald* experience Storke set up law offices in Santa Barbara and from 1913 to 1925 was editorial manager of the Santa Barbara *Daily News*. Thomas M. Storke, *California Editor* (Los Angeles, 1958), pp. 26-27.

Angeles. The other newspapers were the *Star* (morning) owned and edited by Maj. Ben C. Truman;[2] and the *Evening Express*, owned by Tiffany & Paynter, two practical printers, and edited by Col. James J. Ayers.[3]

In politics the *Star* was for the candidate who "whacked up" the best, and the *Express* was avowedly independent. So, until the *Herald* came, the Democratic party in Los Angeles had no reliable newspaper organ. Manifestly Mr. Storke came to fill a long-felt want. The *Star* establishment was located in an old-time adobe residence on Spring Street, a few doors south of Temple; and the *Express*, business office and plant, on the second floor of the old Temple Block, southwest corner. Ten months of strenuous effort on the part of Mr. Storke in filling the Democratic want served to expand his ideas and dissipate his capital. He sold the establishment in August, 1874, to a stock company composed of Judge J. S. Thompson, J. W. Potts, P. Beaudry, F. P. F. Temple, F. G. Gary and M. J. Bixley.[4] Judge Thompson was President of the company, and Theodore Glancey was installed as editor.

[2]The Los Angeles *Star*, southern California's first newspaper, founded in 1851, came under the ownership of Ben C. Truman on July 1, 1873. He remained its editor until 1877; two years later it went bankrupt. William B. Rice, *The Los Angeles Star, 1851-1864*, ed. John W. Caughey (Berkeley, 1947).

[3]The weekly edition of the Los Angeles *Express* ran from 1871 to 1899; the daily from 1871 to 1931, when it was merged with the *Herald*. Tiffany and Co., which founded the *Express*, was composed of George and Jesse Yarnell, George A. Tiffany, John W. Paynter, and Miguel Verelo. Muir Dawson, "Southern California Newspapers, 1851-1876," *Historical Society of Southern California Quarterly*, XXXII (March and June 1950), 29-30.

James J. Ayers came to California in the Gold Rush of 1849 and helped found the San Francisco *Call*. He moved south to Los Angeles only two years before Spalding arrived. He worked on the *Star*, just prior to Ben Truman's accession, and later was editor of the *Express*. For more details, see Ayers, *Gold and Sunshine: Reminiscences of Early California* (Boston, 1922).

The place Los Angeles is hereafter implied in all footnote references to the *Star*, *Herald*, *Express*, or *Times*.

[4]James Wesley Potts (called "Little Potts," "Prophet Potts," and "Uncle Jimmy Potts") tramped his way from Texas to Los Angeles in 1852. His early fruit peddling blossomed into a profitable produce business, and he supposedly introduced the first locally grown sweet potatoes. He was a partner with Beaudry in opening up Temple Street and served on the city council from 1876 to 1878. Spalding in the Los Angeles County Pioneers, *Historical Record and Souvenir* (Los Angeles, 1923), p. 30, called him unkempt and uncouth.

Prudent Beaudry, "a native of Quebec destined to make and lose several fortunes" (Harris Newmark, *Sixty Years in Southern California* [New York, 1926], p. 73), made some money in San Francisco during the Gold Rush, then came south to become, with men like Isaias Hellman and Harris Newmark, one of Los Angeles' most prominent merchants. In the 1850's, Newmark says, Beaudry was making a thousand dollars a month. In 1866 he sold his store to Newmark and engaged thereafter in real-estate development. He was on the city council from 1871 to 1874 and

Under Mr. Glancey's kindly coaching, I soon established a routine of daily calls that gave information of practically everything of public interest that happened in our quiet burg. Judge Gray, the one justice of the peace, had his office in the southeast corner of Temple Block. He tried police cases as well as civil, and the entire business was not sufficient to justify the employment of a clerk. He kept the docket himself, and what more could you ask? He was stout, white-haired, dignified, and in all our acquaintance I never discovered but one flash of humor in him; that was so good that I wished he had indulged oftener. But he probably thought it infra dig for a magistrate.[5]

The District Court and the County Court were in the upper floor of the old Court House, where Bullard Block later stood and now the City Hall. The two tribunals were presided over by Judge Ignacio Sepúlveda and Judge H. K. S. O'Melveny.[6] I rarely ventured into their august presence, as all items respecting their proceedings were to be had in the office of the County Clerk on the ground floor, middle of the building, with a door off Market Street. Wilse [Andrew Wilson] Potts was the ever-popular County Clerk, and Charlie Gould and E. H. Owen were the deputies. The deputies gave me such items as they thought would interest the public, or such as I inquired about, and occasionally when a criminal case of unusual interest was on, lasting into the afternoon, or possibly going over into the next day, I slipped into

mayor for the year following. Leonard J. Rose, Jr., *L. J. Rose of Sunny Slope* (San Marino, Calif., 1959), p. 91, described him as prim and Napoleonic.

Francis Pliny Fisk Temple, five feet four inches (known as "Templito"), came to Los Angeles as a boy of nineteen in 1841. Like a Spanish don, he ranched on the outskirts of town and only later became an active developer and investor. He was city treasurer, 1851-1852, county treasurer in 1876, one of the first Los Angeles county supervisors, and a founder of the Temple and Workman Bank in 1871.

Spalding's dating of Storke's sale to the company is in error. Instead of in August, the *Herald* on March 28, 1874, announced its new joint-stock publishing company and added the name of I. W. Lord to those on the Spalding list. Thomas Storke, *California Editor*, p. 27, said his father was in Los Angeles six months, not ten as Spalding says. This would make his return to Santa Barbara late March or early April.

[5]According to Newmark, William H. Gray was justice of the peace as early as 1871; he was still listed in this office by the directory of Los Angeles for 1875.

(Directories are herein cited with only the year. Those consulted were issued by many different publishers, usually in Los Angeles, and under various titles.)

[6]Ignacio Sepúlveda, an Angeleno by birth and part of an old, highly respected Spanish family, had, before Spalding arrived, already served on the board of education, in the state legislature, and in the county courts, and had become district judge the year before Spalding's account.

Henry Kilpatrick Stuart O'Melveny, "temperate, mild-mannered, and the soul of honor" (Rose, p. 66), served as county judge, 1874-1877. He had practiced law briefly in Sacramento in the Gold Rush era, had served as a circuit judge in Illinois, and had presided over the Los Angeles city council, 1871-1872.

the court room with bated breath, to get a tinge of coloring for my report.

The Sheriff's office was in the northwest corner of the building, ground floor, opening on Spring Street. Billy Rowland was Sheriff, and big, taciturn, kindly old Horace Burdick, clerk and office factotum. What it was proper to know could be got from Horace, and what he did not choose to communicate it was not worth while to try to find out. Billy Rowland never told anything, unless it was an occasional good story to his select coterie of friends. To the reporters he always said, "See Horace."[7]

Charlie Miles, the popular and sometimes festive County Recorder, had his office in the Main Street end of the building, ground floor, and that was the driest department of the county government—so far as news went.[8]

The Supervisors met in a little room opening on Court Street, south side of the building, but their sessions were infrequent, about once a month, I think. Unless the reporter got his tip from the Clerk's office he was liable to miss the Supervisors entirely; and they didn't care.

The city departments were in a long one-story adobe building on Spring Street, corner of Jail Street, afterwards Franklin. The lot in the rear of the city building, extending back to New High Street, was inclosed with a high board fence, and in the middle of the lot, a small, two-story brick building like a block-house, with grated windows, was the jail, or "calaboose," as it was commonly called. It served for both city and county purposes. About the middle of the adobe building on Spring Street there was an open door and a narrow passage-way extending back to the jail yard. The inner end of this passage was guarded by a stout door, with a little peep-hole through it that enabled the jailer to open up sufficiently to inspect any party seeking admission. Jailer Thompson's family occupied the portion of the building from the passage-way south, to Jail Street. North of the passage-way, with an independent doorway off Spring Street, reached by three

[7]William Rowland was city jailer in 1872-1873 and became county sheriff shortly thereafter. Newmark (p. 532) commented on his loss of the position of sheriff in 1882.

[8]In 1875 Charles E. Miles was one of the proprietors of the Los Angeles Pipe Works on Alameda Street. He was an organizer of the volunteer fire brigade, the Thirty-Eights, and later chief engineer of the fire department, 1876-1880. Spalding in his *History*, I, 260, adds a later footnote to Miles's life: "October 12th [1885] Charles E. Miles, County Recorder, was arrested for the embezzlement of $12,000. He paid the money into court, and the charge was dismissed, but he was deposed from his office."

or four steps, was the Council Chamber. This was a room not over fifteen by twenty feet, lighted by the door and one window in front, and a little window, not over two feet square, in the rear, looking into the jail yard. At the north end of the building there was a little office room about ten feet square, for the City Clerk and City Treasurer, provided with a vault for safe storage, having a rather formidable steel door and ponderous lock. It was the only impressive and up-to-date thing in the building. The main room was divided by a railing longitudinally, giving passage to the little office, and furnishing the only available lobby for the public. Behind this railing the august council held its sessions. The council met every Thursday afternoon; and it was a tedious half day for all concerned. I felt the necessity of remaining all through the session, and reporting every transaction, seriatim, as well as giving a digest of the discussions.

The business was transacted in three languages. Don Pedro Vejar, one of the councilmen, could understand only Spanish, and when any matter came to a vote, it had to be explained to him by Mr. Sabichi, another member. Don José Mascarel could understand only French, and it was necessary for Mr. Beaudry to give him an explanation of the question, and a running digest of the arguments on both sides. Then the ballot was taken, and I noticed that Don Pedro always voted as Mr. Sabichi did, and Don José always voted as Mr. Beaudry did. From this I judged that the translations were effective. This rather laborious process gave me opportunity to write up my notes, and I generally managed to have my copy ready to turn in to the printer, subheads and all, as soon as I reached the office.[9]

The depot of the Southern Pacific railway was at the foot of Commercial Street on Alameda. The only road operating then was the line between that point and Wilmington. The depot was a long wooden building, with a high platform along the Alameda Street side and on the Commercial Street end. The latter was for the reception of freight from teams, and it was trucked through

[9]Frank (Francisco) Sabichi, born in Los Angeles but educated in England, returned to his native city in 1860, practiced law, developed land, and served frequently on the city council. In 1874 he was council president.

José Mascarel, "a powerfully-built French sea-captain" (Newmark, p. 62), had been in Los Angeles since 1844 and held the office of mayor in 1865 and city councilman off and on from 1864 to 1882. Mascarel spoke some English but was never adept at it.

Other members of the city council in 1874 (aside from Prudent Beaudry, already discussed) were Edward Huber, Jacob F. Gherkins, Julian Chavez, William H. Workman, Eulogio de Celis, Henry Dockweiler, and Julian Valdez. There was no Pedro Vejar, and Spalding has probably confused this name with either Chavez or Valdez.

the building or around on the platform to be loaded on cars. Per contra, incoming freight was unloaded on the Alameda Street side, and trucked around to the Commercial Street end for delivery. Incidentally, this same platform served for passenger traffic also. Remi Nadeau's freight line, with big "prairie schooners" and trailers, drawn by twelve or fourteen-mule teams, was in full operation, bringing in bullion from the Beaudry & Belshaw mine, near Independence, Inyo county, and hauling back supplies; rates, ten cents a pound.[10] The bullion came in great pigs, weighing two or three hundred pounds each, containing a percentage of silver, but the bulk lead. The weight of the bars constituted the chief insurance against robbery, I imagine, for they were too heavy for Vasquez and his gang to carry away. It was not an unusual thing to see those bars stacked like cordwood on the depot platform.

The building was an all-purpose affair. At the Commercial Street end there was space for the reception and delivery of freight; then, on the Alameda Street side in the corner was a small waiting room and ticket office for passengers. Then came the office of Col. E. E. ("Ned") Hewitt, the Superintendent, and a clerk or two.[11] It was a small force altogether, but it had only a small system to operate, and got through the business in first-class shape. Next came the telegraph office, about ten feet square, presided over by Tom McCaffrey, the only operator, with Nat Furman as understudy, office-boy and messenger.[12] Tom McCaffrey was my right bower. Having a pretty good "nose for news" himself, and being not over-crowded with work, he kept me posted on things happening anywhere along the line, the arrival of ships and cargoes at the port, and even news from Inyo county brought in by the freighters. I made a daily call on Tom, and he was long-suffering and patient.

I have thus outlined my daily routine for newsgathering;

[10]"Remi Nadeau's line of freighting teams took care of the traffic between the two points. The wagon was a ponderous affair, popularly designated a 'prairie schooner', and behind this was drawn a trailer of equal capacity. A team of fourteen to sixteen mules was required to haul the twin carriers. The lead mules were equipped with strings of bells attached to their high arching hames, and when a long train passed through the town everybody knew it." Spalding, *History*, I, 255.

[11]Eldridge Edwards Hewitt, a California '49er who got sidetracked into Los Angeles, worked for Phineas Banning at Wilmington, became superintendent of the Los Angeles and San Pedro Railroad in 1870, and when that road was absorbed by the Southern Pacific in 1873 remained as its agent.

[12]Thomas McCaffrey (also spelled McCaffary or McCaffery in Los Angeles directories) later became a train dispatcher for the Southern Pacific.

Nat may have been the son of George R. Furman, the freight clerk at the depot, referred to in the directory of 1875 and in Ayers, *Gold and Sunshine*, p. 259.

other things were caught on the fly. Any excitement in police circles, any alarm of fire, any runaway team made such a sensation in the little burg that I was sure to get hold of it promptly. It did not require very long for me to get acquainted with a lot of folks, and to know who the others were, even if I did not have a speaking acquaintance. In those days, too, people took pains to tell a reporter about various happenings; they seemed to take a friendly interest in him and liked to see things that they had suggested come out in the fresh damp paper the next morning. So it was not long before I began to feel myself in the swim, and that I was a real factor in the affairs of town.

Merced Theater, owned by Wm. Abbott, was on Main Street, in a three-story brick building, a few doors below [actually adjoining] the Pico House. The auditorium was a long, narrow, badly lighted, illy ventilated room on the second floor. It had a small stage at the inner end, a fairly high ceiling, and had been finished with some regard to ornament, but was old and shabby when I first saw it. As a revenue producer it could not have been much of a factor, for Merced Theater was dark most of the time. If something was pulled off there once a month, it was a good average. Los Angeles was so far away from any line of travel, so difficult and expensive of access, that no regular troupes came through, and if anything in the dramatic or musical way appeared it was furnished by local talent, or by some remnant of a stranded company endeavoring to make a stake to get out of the country. The only exception to this sort of thing that I remember was when the graduating exercises of the first class from the Los Angeles High School were held in the place. That was a gala affair, and old Merced Theater was packed "from orchestra chairs to balcony"—or would have been if there had been a balcony.[13]

Whenever anything did happen at Merced Theater, it was, of course, a grand occasion for the newspaper reporter. To walk up to the doorkeeper with a nonchalant air and flash upon him a ticket with "Complimentary" written across its face in red ink,

[13]"A little below the Pico House was Merced theater . . . . It was a three-story brick with ornamental front, devoted to some commercial purpose on the ground floor, and a stairway, fairly broad, leading to the hall on the second floor. The Abbott family lived in the third. Whenever something was going on in the theater there was sure to be a crowd of Abbott children stationed on the upper stairway, and scurrying across the landing to take in as much of the excitement as they could get free. Old man Abbott, thin and of rather nervous temperament, always more or less unshorn and unshaven, was apt to be in evidence somewhere about the premises, busy about one thing or another, and Mrs. Abbott, a middle-aged Spanish woman, of dominating presence, sometimes appeared and took command of the children. The hall was largely a family affair." Spalding, *History*, I, 185-186.

or, perchance, merely to hand him your personal card, with "Herald" in moderate sized type down in one corner; to acknowledge his deferential salute by bowing in a kindly way yourself; to then be specially introduced to the head usher, and by him escorted to a preferred seat away up in front, or at a table expressly prepared for the press; and then, when you felt that a great many eyes were upon you, to take your seat in a perfectly cool and deliberate way, shifting your note-book, so as to have it handy at a moment's call—to do all this, I say, was glory enough for any man living, and there are doubtless many dead who never achieved anything equal to it.

But "pride," the good book says, "goeth before destruction." One day I looked in at the *Herald* office at the usual hour—ten o'clock —and went out for my regular morning round. When I returned about noon I found a stranger there who seemed very much at home. He was a dapper little fellow, with the reddest of hair that curled down upon his head, and his whole appearance seemed sandy. Bustling up to me, he said, with a fetching smile, "Is there anything that I can do for you, Sir?"

Then and there I knew that something dreadful had happened. I was completely nonplussed, and stammered out, "I—— I—— don't know; I—— used to work here—this morning."

"Oh, yes," he said, perpetrating that same smile again, "you are the young man who is getting items; that's all right; you can keep right on."

Whether I fainted and fell on the floor, and had to be carried to the drug store next door, or what did happen, I have no means of knowing, for my mind is a blank on this part of the evidence. I only know that I did "keep right on," and was humbly thankful that I was not of enough consequence to be kicked out. It is superfluous to say that the *Herald* had undergone another revolution, and up to the incident just recorded, I had been oblivious to the mighty internal throes. It seems that Judge R. M. Widney and some of his associates had acquired stock enough to give them control, and they had wrested the management from Judge Thompson and his crowd. Sam, Judge Widney's brother, had been temporarily installed in the office, to tide things over. Hence the smile and the episode.[14]

But my zeal in the newspaper field has got me ahead of the

[14]Robert Maclay Widney left Ohio and gypsied about the West during the 1850's before settling in Los Angeles in 1868. Newmark (p. 401) called him one of the first real-estate agents in town, but he had also practiced law from the start. He was involved in countless development schemes, including newspapers and street railways.

chronological order of my story. Fred and I staid only a day or two at the United States Hotel. When Mr. Glancey found that we were in quest of a room he offered to rent us one in his home at a modest price. He and his young wife were occupying an adobe house on Main Street, between Second and Third. That is to say, Second and Third streets had not yet been cut through, but it was about that locality. The house was one of the luxurious old Spanish homes which Mr. Glancey had rented furnished. On the outside it was plain enough, but within it was home-like and delightful. In our room we had elegant old-fashioned mahogany "four-poster" bedsteads with the finest of bedding, each bed inclosed with lace curtains and valances. The other furniture of the room was on an equally elaborate scale, and the whole house, in fact, was an old-fashioned dream. The Glanceys warmed to a former Galesburg boy and his chum, and made us feel at home, inviting us occasionally to a Sunday dinner, and to spend the evening with them. Fred and I considered that we were playing to the greatest of good fortune. But it was too good to last. The revolution in the *Herald* office ended all that. Glancey moved up to Santa Barbara, where he edited the *Press* for a year or two. In a hot political campaign, a man named Gray with a record behind him was a candidate for some office, I think the judgeship. Glancey exposed and fought him, and he demonstrated the correctness of the editorial position by assassinating the editor at his desk. Poor Glancey! he died a martyr to professional duty. He was a thorough gentleman, a good newspaper man, a man of fine instincts.[15] And the sweet little wife; I felt sorriest for her.

We next went to room and board with a printer named Harris in a brick building on Aliso Street, and there our quarters were crude and humble enough to do penance for our temporary elegance in the old Spanish home.[16] But we passed some happy months there just the same. Afterward we found more desirable quarters with Mrs. [A. J.] Clapp, a widow with three children, in a cottage on Spring Street near Third, where the Douglas Building now stands. We boarded with "Mam" Backman in the

[15]Clarence Gray was a nominee for district attorney in Santa Barbara. Glancey's editorial that had such unfortunate consequences was written during the fall of 1880 in connection with a summarization of the qualifications of the candidates. Glancey had been succinct regarding Gray: "For District Attorney, a man who goes by the name of Gray, with how many aliases it is impossible to say, was nominated. The charity of our silence is more than he can expect." Quoted in Storke, *California Editor*, p. 95.

[16]The directory of 1875 listed S. T. Harris, a printer, residing on First Street between Los Angeles and Alameda.

old Schumacher home, on Spring Street between First and Jail streets.

Andy Lawrence came up from San Diego shortly after Fred and I did. His aristocratic military acquaintance had not helped him into anything whereby he could earn a living. We three were chums again in the humble Aliso Street lodgings. Fred and Andy found it rather difficult to "catch on" at first, and after trying everything that looked like a prospect, they used to take long rambles in the environs of the town, and even some distance into the country, in order that they might not get themselves classed as habitual loafers. Finally Fred struck a short job with John Goldsworthy, the surveyor, and after laying out some lots in one of the new additions, went to Holcomb Valley with a party to survey mines.[17] Lawrence struck some temporary work that helped to tide him along. Later he came into a little money by inheritance, which he invested in a tobacco-growing enterprise at Gilroy, where he blew it all in, together with a year of hard work.[18]

Fred at last settled into a permanent and satisfactory place as secretary for Prudent Beaudry, a man of wealth and enterprise, who was doing a great deal for Los Angeles. Mr. Beaudry subdivided and placed on the market all the hilly portion of the city on the northwest, graded his own streets, built his own system of water-works to supply the high lands, constructed the Temple Street cable railway, and made everything move that he took hold of. In this sort of work Fred was well calculated to shine, and he soon became invaluable to his boss. Later Mr. Beaudry was elected Mayor, and Fred served him as official secretary through his term, as well as taking care of his diversified private interests. Fred could write a message for the Mayor, as well as operate his railroad and water-works.[19] After beating around a

[17]John C. Goldsworthy was city surveyor and engineer in 1872 and city surveyor in 1878-1879. Throughout the seventies he had an office in the Temple Block. Holcomb Valley in the San Bernardino Mountains was a center of gold activity beginning in 1860.

[18]On June 23, 1874, the *Herald* reported that A.M. Lawrence was leaving for San Francisco, from which place he hoped to proceed to Gilroy to raise tobacco.

[19]"At the further end [of the very short Republic Street] stands a trim, newly painted two-story building that is a landmark. In the seventies and eighties it belonged to Prudent Beaudry, and there, on the ground floor, he kept his office, his front windows commanding a view down the whole length of Republic street and across Main to the Pico House. In that office, capacious enough, and elegantly appointed for those times, Prudent Beaudry, with his Secretary of State, Fred Wood, presided and shaped the destiny of all the northwestern, hilly, portion of the city." Spalding, *History*, I, 192.

good deal, Andy Lawrence finally settled into his groove as secretary for the Board of Trade when it was first established [1883], and proved a great success. But I am getting away from my newspaper story.

When Judge Widney's crowd got possession of the *Herald*, they inducted as manager Dana C. Pearson, an elderly man, long, lank and ostentatiously pious. The last named characteristic was borne in upon us by the fact that he was everlastingly lecturing us on moral and religious topics, and the boys resented it. First they called him "Bible-back," but finally settled down to "Aunt Polly." I doubt if he had enjoyed any previous newspaper experience, or he would have known better how to go about it; but he tried to make it appear, without exactly saying so, that he was an old hand at the newspaper game.[20]

> Oh, what a tangled web we weave,
> When first we practice to deceive.

"Aunt Polly" made all sorts of blunders, and was heartily laughed at behind his back; but we all listened respectfully to his lectures. One of his first executive acts was to install a book-keeper. The one selected for this position was a young fellow named George Safford. I felt a little twinge of disappointment at this because I regarded myself as an experienced book-keeper, and would have been glad to undertake the work in addition to my other duties. But George Safford was a boy whom I had met at "Mam" Backman's boarding house—a fine young fellow, and we were already quite chummy. After putting in his time at odds and ends the first day, George and I got together for a quiet talk, and he said: "Look here, Billy, I am in a devil of a scrape. I don't know a blamed thing about book-keeping, but I've got to hold this job down somehow—I've just got to." After indulging in a good laugh at the situation, I said, "Well, don't you worry about it; keep a stiff upper lip, and don't let Aunt Polly know, and I'll pull you through." So, at odd and sequestered hours I gave him the fundamentals of double-entry book-keeping; saw that he was headed right, and made no mistakes in entries or posting. He was an apt pupil, wrote a good hand, and had a business air that would command anybody's confidence. He skated along beautifully, and I doubt whether Aunt Polly or anybody

[20]The *Herald* on June 10, 1874, announced the appointment of Pearson, who had been "for a long time connected with the large Publishing house of J. H. Carmany & Co., in San Francisco, as editor of *The Dial*, *The West*, Pacific Coast editor of *Crofutt's Western World*. He was also correspondent of the *Resources of California*."
The ensuing quotation is from Sir Walter Scott, *Marmion*, Canto VI.

else in the office suspected the thin ice under his skates. Then and there George and I cemented a life-long friendship.

"Aunt Polly" did not last very long. Just how he faded out I have no clear recollection. But a good many things occurred in the *Herald* office that I knew nothing about until after they had happened, and a thing or two, it seems, that even the manager didn't know.

A few months later George Safford obtained a position that paid better, and then the books were given over to me, in addition to my other duties, and I was able thereby to warp my salary up to $25 a week. Safford subsequently made his mark in Los Angeles as one of the founders of the California Truck Company and a heavy operator in real estate, accumulating a considerable fortune before his untimely death.[21]

Our next editor was J. M. Bassett, a man of about fifty years, who had been trained to the business from his youth, who had seen service on the press of the upper part of the state, some of it in San Francisco, and who was conversant with politics and everything else that an editor ought to know, and more.[22] A greater contrast to "Aunt Polly" could not have been found. He was big and burly, weighing about one hundred and eighty pounds, and set up like a prize-fighter. He wore a full beard, short and stubby, and his hair curled in a bellicose way. He was a vigorous, epigrammatic writer, and had a way of saying things that made them seem fresh and interesting; in other words, he wrote editorials that everybody wanted to read. In the office we were delighted with the change. While Bassett left no doubt in anybody's mind that he was boss, there was still a rough bonhomie that made everybody like him, and he could utter a full-mouthed "Damn," with a smile that was very fetching. I never forgot a lesson he gave me one day when he brought one of my reports back to me, with a long blue-pencil mark through two or three of the choicest sentences. "Whenever you think you have

[21]Safford established the California Truck Company in 1884 with Edward H. O'Melveny, his brother-in-law and a son of H. K. S. O'Melveny.

[22]James M. Bassett was actually editor before Pearson became business manager, and he apparently remained editor through and after Pearson's tenure, which ended in early August. The *Herald* of April 16, 1874, referred to its new editor, Bassett, as having been recently connected with the San Francisco press and before that, "several years ago," editor of the Stockton *Republican*. The *Express* of Jan. 9, 1878, reprinted a story concerning Bassett from the San Francisco *Mail* under the heading "A Man We Know." Bassett was described sitting in the office of the *Portico* (circulation, 30 per week) with a forty-two-inch chest, muscular development which a prize fighter would envy, and black whiskers sandy next to his skin. He was made to appear a pompous windbag.

written something smart," he said, "take your own pencil and cross it out; it'll save time." And he smiled at me in a way that took away all of the sting of his speech. Nevertheless I could not help thinking that he did not treat his own editorials that way. But probably my callow sense of levity, which was too prone to crop out in wrong places, needed to be held down.

The front part of the *Herald* office, facing Spring Street, was divided into little cribs, or stalls, by half-high partitions, forming offices about ten feet square. There were two of these offices on each side, and a narrow passage between them, leading to the mechanical department in the rear. The front crib on the left hand side as you entered the main door was the business office, where I combined the duties of book-keeper and city editor, and across the narrow aisle, in front, was the sanctum, where Mr. Bassett presided.

One day a smart looking young fellow came in and inquired for the editor. It was the regular thing for people to ask for the editor when they had any business to transact with the paper, and I answered, off-hand, "I'm one of them; what can I do for you?" The young fellow stepped quickly inside the door, and said, "Then I've got a matter to settle with you, right now," picking up a heavy ruler from the desk. I really thought I was a goner; but just at that instant came Mr. Bassett, rolling ponderously out of his office, and surprising my angry visitor on his left flank. I had never before been so glad to see a man that looked like a prize-fighter. Well, the matter ended without my getting a licking for something which had appeared in the paper, and for which I may or may not have deserved a licking. Later I found that our caller was a theatrical man whose sensitive corns had been tramped on. But that episode taught me a lesson—not to be too ready to assume a responsibility until I knew what it was.

In the course of my early newspaper life I must have received calls from a dozen or more angry men, who came to the office for the express purpose of whipping the editor or reporter, or somebody. When I got an early inkling of the caller's state of mind, I always invited him suavely to take a seat, and I would talk to him in a minute, as soon as I had finished my sentence; and I got very busy on that sentence. By the time I turned about, and asked how I could be of service to him, he was more than half mollified, and ready to talk matters over in a reasonable way. I went through all sorts of exciting and angry campaigns, and sometimes when things were particularly squally, had a revolver tucked under a pile of newspapers on my desk, but I never was put to the necessity of drawing it in self defence, and never got a licking. Once a big Scotchman came into the office, angry through and through, blustering in the broadest of brogues, and declaring that he was going to "whop" somebody. "Then, Sandy," I said, "ye might as weel begin, and whop me, for I'm Sco-otch mesel'." After that he was easy to manage.

Once when the political ring that dominated city politics had called a mass-meeting in one of the court rooms, I attended, and, in the capacity of citizen rather than reporter, made a motion of some sort that seemed not to accord with the pre-arranged plan. As a clear majority voted in favor of my motion, the gang found nothing better to do than bolt the meeting with more or less disorder. When I came down from the hall one of the select group, a man of violent temper and a bully, confronted me with a revolver in his hand, and proceeded to tell what he thought of me. My back was against the building, and there seemed nothing to do but stand and take the tirade, which I did without uttering a word. After the fellow had flourished his weapon about my head to his satisfaction, and had grown tired of damning me up one side and down the other, his attention was diverted by some of his friends, and I slipped out of the crowd and hurried over to our office, which was just across the street. My first intention was to get my revolver and go back, and have it out with him on equal terms. But, when I reached the office, a more sane thought began to come, and I said to myself, "How foolish that would be. The way to beat that crowd is to expose them." So I obtained a brass ring from the job office—the kind we used for printing drug labels—and had the heading of my report set in and around that ring, so that all would show up together in a sort of mosaic. In the report I exposed the plans of the political ring; what they had set out to do, and how they had failed to accomplish it, and had demoralized the meeting and broken it up. My revenge was full and satisfactory. The combination was busted for that election, at least.[23]

After Mr. Bassett got comfortably seated in the editorial chair, things went on at a handsome clip for several months. Under a strong and consistent editorship, the *Herald* was actually making headway and beginning to command the confidence and respect of the public. Business was looking up in the community

[23]The available files of the *Herald* do not reveal this article. It probably was printed during November or early December 1874, prior to the election of December 7 when Beaudry was elected mayor. During that period the *Herald* constantly referred to the "ring," and to the *Express* as the "ring" organ.

also; new enterprises and land subdivisions were coming to the front and required advertising, and we derived our share of the benefits. About this time Dan Freeman launched his subdivision scheme of the Centinela ranch, which included a large acreage where the Soldiers' Home is now located, extending thence to the ocean. Dan was a good advertiser, and I made a trip or two over the ranch and told the public what a wonderful property it was.[24]

Santa Monica was also subdivided and placed on the market as a seaside resort. The first substantial movement by the company was to build a small hotel a block or two back from the beach, and when that was completed, it was opened to the public with a grand flare. It was the only building in the place. But the projectors of this scheme had been so exceedingly short-sighted as not to advertise in the *Herald*. We therefore looked rather coldly upon it, and were disposed to side with conservative citizens who considered the enterprise hair-brained and reckless. In preparation for the grand opening the company had sent down some potted trees and shrubs which were transplanted about the hotel to improve the grounds and give the place an atmosphere of attractiveness. That sort of thing was novel, and smacked so much of catchpenny device that our editor could not restrain his own disposition to say "something smart," and he fired off some editorials that made the company appear very ridiculous.[25]

It was too early, however, for boom enterprises. The Centinela scheme, which we favored, proved a flat failure; and the Santa Monica scheme, which we ridiculed, was just a stand-off. Santa Monica lots did not sell worth a cent, although the company held its ground, and operated the hotel, probably at a considerable loss. A few cottages were built in the neighborhood of the hotel.

One calm day Los Angeles was much surprised and sat up to take notice of an article which appeared in the *Herald*, exposing and denouncing the system of the Los Angeles Water Company. It represented that the supply, which everybody depended upon for domestic uses, was brought down from its source in the river

[24]Daniel Freeman had been led to California in 1873 by Charles Nordhoff's travel account. He bought 25,000 acres of the Centinela Ranch, which he stocked with sheep and planted with orchards. In 1887 a part of the ranch was subdivided into the suburb of Inglewood.

[25]Col. Robert S. Baker and Senator John P. Jones were behind the first operations. Newmark (p. 479) attended the auction sale of July 15, 1875, and succumbed to the "pyrotechnical efforts" of the auctioneer, who described Santa Monica as the "Zenith City by the Sunset Sea." Hotel Arcadia was built by Senator Jones; Jones's own home later became the Miramar Hotel. The stories to which Spalding refers, about the opening celebrations and their failure, appeared in the *Herald*, July 16 and 17, 1875.

bed, opposite Los Feliz ranch, in an open ditch, and impounded in an open reservoir; that the ditch and reservoir were covered with a green vegetable growth (algae), a breeding place for mosquitoes and all sorts of animal life and germs; that, in short, the water was unfit to drink, and liable to cause an epidemic. This article no doubt told the truth, and gave a needed warning; but it was as much of a surprise to me as to any outsider. It had probably been prepared by somebody not connected with the paper, and handed to our editor, and he had the nerve to run it on its merits. It was the first real newspaper sensation that the sleepy old town had ever had.

The next day we received notice of a libel suit for ten thousand dollars against the *Herald*, brought by the water company. I was glad then that it was not some of my smartness that had got the paper into trouble. Bassett didn't seem to care much; he knew he was in the right of the contest; he had nothing personally at stake, and anyhow the whole newspaper establishment wasn't worth ten thousand dollars. Why should he worry?

But the enemy worked a flank attack that none of us were prepared for. Uncle Jimmy Potts, one of the original stockholders of the *Herald*, was employed by members of the water company to slip around quietly and pick up enough stock to give control of the paper. When this became known to us, we realized that the jig was up, so far as the fight on the water company went. Bassett probably made the best compromise he could, which was to save his own bacon. In about a week I was sent out to inspect the reservoir and ditch, and reported truthfully that both had been thoroughly cleaned. I was sure of this because I saw the green scum, which had been taken off and was piled up in profusion all along the banks. In due time the libel suit was dismissed; of course there was nothing in it for the water company to get a judgment against its own newspaper. As to the green scum, I expect it formed again in a little time, as it always had done and always will, when water is exposed to sunshine. But we did not hunt for green scum after that.[26]

Matters went along much the same after our latest revolution; in fact it had made less internal commotion than any of its prede-

[26]The earliest *Herald* story on impure water after Spalding's arrival was Oct. 18, 1874. A reference to Potts becoming "the agent of certain parties to clandestinely buy up a majority of the stock of the *Herald*, and place that institution in the hands of men whose objects were opposed to the interests of the city" appeared in the *Express*, July 30, 1875. Similar stories, including foul water, algae, and the cleaning of the reservoir, appeared in Spalding's columns in the *Express*, July 23, 24, and 28, 1877.

cessors, and outsiders could hardly tell that there had been a revolution, so smoothly had it been pulled off. A few months afterwards the *Herald* fell into a great piece of good fortune. The Sacramento *Union*, after a long and ineffectual fight against the Southern Pacific railroad monopoly, had been acquired by the "octopus," as we were wont to call it, in much the same way that the *Herald* had been taken over by the water company. Under a new management the *Union* office had been given a thorough overhauling, and a new press installed. The discarded press, a lumbering old cast-iron structure, requiring lots of power to operate, was shipped down to us, freight free, by the railroad company. It was an out-and-out gift. Whether the railroad company did this from spontaneous goodness of heart, or because they wanted to help a poor but honest newspaper, or because they thought it might be a good thing to have an anchor to leeward in these southern waters, I did not ascertain. I only know that the press came, free of charge, and was duly set up in our office. Incidentally, Bassett told me, as book-keeper, not to enter it up as an asset of the concern.

We had in our composing room a couple of girl-apprentices, who were learning to set type and become full-fledged printers. I think it was one of "Aunt Polly's" fool ideas that had held over. They were smart girls, and were learning fast enough, but as time wore on they became great favorites of our editor-in-chief; so much so in fact, that a good third of working hours was passed by them in the sanctum. It happened occasionally that a visitor, opening his door without warning, would find one of the girls seated on the editor's lap, and the other running her fingers through his curly locks. I suppose they made a good deal of him in their artless, girly way. I felt rather sorry for Mrs. Bassett, who was a good, motherly old soul, and I felt sorry for Bassett, too, because I really liked him, and knew that such goings-on couldn't last long. And they didn't.

Information of the girl episodes probably reached the owners of the paper, and no doubt somebody remonstrated with Bassett. One thing led to another, and finally they got to fussing about that press. Bassett claimed that it was a gift to him personally, and the directors held that it was the property of the concern. They appealed to the correspondence, books and records, and found that *the press had been duly entered among the assets.*[27]

---

[27]It is not clear here who entered the press on the books. It is, however, not unlike Spalding to have done so, considering it the right thing to do, in spite of Bassett's orders.

Then our fourth revolution was on, and the editor-in-chief, the foreman and the two apprentice girls went.

The management of the paper was then placed in my hands.[28] It was a catch-as-catch-can proposition for a political editor. Probably I might have assumed the editorial chair, had I been so disposed, but I did not regard myself as competent to fill it; certainly I had enough on my hands, rustling for the local columns, keeping the books, making collections, and managing things generally, without assuming any more duties. And there seemed to be nobody available to relieve me of any part of my routine. Besides, I assumed that the directors would want to pick out their own editor.

The first man whom they selected for the place was Gen. J. M. Baldwin, a brother of Leon McL. Baldwin, owner of Los Feliz ranch. Gen. Baldwin was a typical southern gentleman, an ex-Confederate officer, a man of all-round education, and was always immaculately dressed.[29] He was a personal friend, I think, of some member of the water company. How his selection came about I do not know, but can easily imagine that in an off-hand way the suggestion was made, "Why can't you take it, General? You're an educated man, and can write beautiful English. Why, it's a snap—only a column or so every day, and you can write about anything—anything. And by God, Sir, you would be an ornament to the establishment."

So General Baldwin came. The first day he ornamented the establishment, and filled his column satisfactorily. The second

---

[28]This was July 13, 1876.

Spalding kept a personal diary, which he sometimes called his "red book," from Nov. 25, 1875, to Aug. 21, 1878. (It is in the possession of Mrs. Helen Groff and is hereafter referred to as Diary.) In his entry for April 13, 1876, Spalding recounted his first full-fledged editorial experience a few months prior to assuming the management of the paper:

"A general flare up in the office. Col. Peel, who was acting editor in the absence of Bassett, had a clash with the management and was relieved. The bone of contention was the newly appointed Board of Public Works and its support by the paper.

"Hancock Johnston, the President of the company, then came to me and gave the editorial charge of the paper into my hands. I employed [A. T.?] Hawley as City Editor and went into the job with all the energy I could muster but not without some misgivings. This is my first experiment at real editorial work and the opportunity has been thrust upon me almost without a moment's notice. My first editorial is entitled 'The American Experiment.' It was written first but held over until Sunday morning for publication."

[29]John M. Baldwin, of the real-estate firm of Baldwin and Beane, was city surveyor for four months in 1875, deputy county recorder in 1883-1884, and city superintendent of streets in 1888.

day there was no abatement of the ornamentation, but the column was only two-thirds filled. The third day he was at his desk in due time, but something seemed to hang fire. After pondering a long time, he went out for a little turn, probably to stir up his thoughts. You know how it is with this perverse thinking apparatus of ours. When you want a thought to come right away, it is often like a shy kitten. Everything may be all ready for it and you call, "Kitty, kitty, kitty," in the most amiable and persistent manner, but the infernal thing just won't come. Well, I imagine it was much that way with the General. In a little time he resumed his seat and also resumed his pondering. The kitty was evidently slow about coming. Then he concluded to go after it again, and bring it in by force if need be. So an hour or two or three was employed in alternate ponderings and sallies, and at last somebody passing the office noticed the General at his desk, his head down on his outstretched arms, fast asleep. He had gone after the kitty two or three times too many. The next day he resigned his editorship and we filled the editorial column with reprint.

After that we had for a time a regular all-round printer and back-east country newspaper man, Randall H. Hewitt (father of Judge Leslie R. Hewitt), whom I conscripted from the job office. He didn't have to chase the kitty at all, but was always ready with his copy, and could lend a hand at the job printing when the boys were pressed.[30]

The newspaper quarters comprised a store room about 30 x 100 feet in area. That was more space than the *Herald* had any use for, so it took as sub-tenants three other papers: *La Cronica*, Spanish; the *Süd Californische Post*, German; and *L'Union Nouvelle*, French. We also took care of our own child, the *Republican*. These were weekly publications, and in our abundant space we accommodated their offices and mechanical plants, and the printing was done on the *Herald* press.[31] Even if somewhat mixed, the arrangement was mutually advantageous, and since the interests were so diverse that they never infringed on each others' territory, so far as patronage went, and the conductors of the several

---

[30]Randall Hewitt had been a newspaperman in Olympia, Washington, before he had come to Los Angeles in 1876. Spalding, *History*, III, 116.

The remainder of this chapter was written separately by Spalding and was inserted by him in only the Groff copy of the "Autobiography."

[31]*La Cronica* was the third Spanish newspaper in Los Angeles, 1872-ca.1892. *Süd Californische Post*, the second German paper in Los Angeles, began in 1874. *L'Union*, the first French paper in the city, and the *Republican* both lasted from 1876 to 1879.

papers were uniformly good natured, we got along like four chums in a bed.

The *Herald* also had a job printing plant that entered into the general melange. Mr. [E. F.] Teodoli was the proprietor and Pastor and Eulogio de Celis in turn the editors of the Spanish paper; Conrad Jacoby owned and conducted the German, and P. Ganée the French. Ganée sometimes got excited and sputtered a little, but as we couldn't understand him, nothing ever came of it.[32]

In the course of my frugal management of the *Herald* it occurred to me that, while we were pretty full as things stood, there was still room to take on something more. In a little wooden lean-to at the back of the building there was an old-fashioned upright boiler—some relic of a threshing outfit, I think—and an engine of six or seven horsepower, always frightfully dirty, but able-bodied and reliable most of the time. Our "power plant" operated a Taylor cylinder press that printed the newspapers, and two or three small job presses. We sometimes boasted rather airily that ours was the only printing establishment in Los Angeles operated by steam power. It seemed to me that this constituted a rather strong hold on the business of the community, as well as being a credit to the city, and we ought to make the most of it. I therefore resolved that our "steam power" should not loaf away any part of its valuable time.

The *Express*, owned by Tiffany & Paynter and edited by Col. J. J. Ayers, was located on the second floor of Temple Block, southwest corner, diagonally opposite our establishment. The *Express* was independent in politics; the *Herald* pronouncedly Democratic.

The *Star*, owned and edited by Maj. Ben C. Truman, was located in a one-story adobe building, midway between our office and Temple Street. The house—evidently an old-time Mexican residence of considerable pretensions in its day—was almost flush with and nearly aligned the street, its eaves to the front, and you went up a few steps to reach the door. This, without any material change in its interior arrangement, had been converted to the uses of the newspaper. An old-time entrance hall was the

---

[32]Pierre Ganée succeeded Frédéric C. de Mondran as editor of *L'Union*, probably late in 1876. When *L'Union Nouvelle* began in 1879 following the demise of *L'Union*, Ganée edited the new journal and did so until his death in 1902. Clifford H. Bissell, "The French Language Press in California," *California Historical Society Quarterly*, XXXIX (Dec. 1960), 329, 342.

A sentence which repeats earlier material has been omitted from the beginning of this paragraph.

business office; a small living room adjoining, with a window looking out upon Spring Street, was the editorial room; back of both, in what had evidently been dining-room and kitchen, were the composing and press rooms. It might be said of the establishment that it was compact and not very inconvenient. In politics the *Star* was a free-lance.

The Mirror job printing office, Yarnell & Caystile proprietors, was in the second floor of the old Downey Block, southwest corner, facing Temple and New High streets. It was the only distinctively job printing concern in town, and the *Mirror*, a folio about the size of a foolscap sheet, was issued weekly as an advertisement for the business. It claimed to have a subscription price, but must have had very few subscribers, for it was distributed gratis. Jesse Yarnell was ubiquitous, known by everybody, and popular. In memory I have a distinct picture of him— tall, angular, with a merry banter for everybody, a bundle of *Mirrors* under one arm, handing out a paper and saying, "Here, read this, the only live newspaper in Los Angeles."[33] Jesse was an ardent advocate of temperance, and such a man was sure to be regarded as peculiar in those times. "It takes cranks to make the world go round," he would say. He was one of the pillars of Merrill Lodge, Good Templars.[34] As the *Mirror* never failed to have something to say for the cause, it came in time to be considered the official organ of the temperance propagandists. But aside from this serious purpose, the *Mirror* made room for a little spicy reprint, and from time to time presented contributed articles that were worth while. I particularly remember a series of this sort called "The Col. Blove Papers." They were written by Col. Jim Howard, a prominent attorney, a man of intellectuality and

[33]Spalding in a deleted section of the "Autobiography" called Yarnell "the most imperturbable man I ever knew," and he once printed in the *Express*, Feb. 15, 1878, a valentine jingle to Yarnell:

> They tell me you have signed the pledge—
> Have joined the Murphyites;
> That wearing a blue-ribbon badge
> Is one of your delights.
> Now, Jess, my boy, pray have a care
> In your new rank and station,
> Lest you should somehow, unaware,
> Disgrace the Irish nation.

Yarnell and Thomas Caystile had set up their job printing shop in 1872; they began publication of the weekly *Mirror* the following year.

[34]This was a temperance society, which Spalding himself later joined for a short period.

culture, who wielded the most incisive pen in our bailiwick, not excepting those of the real editors.[35]

The community of that time was irretrievably Democratic— not that everybody voted the same ticket at all times, but the great preponderance was that way in National and State elections. There was no regular organization of any party but the Democratic. In city and county elections we generally divided on preference for candidates or some big local issue, such as which bank should hold the public funds, or something like that. Then the line of battle would be between the regular cohorts (the stronger party having captured the convention or party machine) and the Antis, calling themselves Independents or Reformers party, or what not.

I remember an election of that character when I observed a well-known and affluent citizen on his way to the center of activity with his pockets bulging, and manifestly heavy. The polling place was in the old Court House, on the Court Street side. Our affluent friend made his headquarters in the office of the County Recorder, at the Main Street end of the same building, and did business. A crowd of Mexican paisanos in single file was marshaled through the office, and as they passed, each was handed a ticket and a silver dollar. The dollar he put in his pocket, and the ticket he held in his hand as an evidence of good faith. The file proceeded out the front door, and around the corner to the polls. There were trusted lieutenants at various points and angles along the line of march, to see that everything was conducted in due form, and the ballots were deposited without a hitch. It is hardly necessary to add that our affluent friend won the election, "hands down." As I was new to the game and had no fear of the powers that were, I took note of the procedure, and in the next morning's *Herald* published a circumstantial account of it, without comment.[36] That was a bit of audacity that had not been known before, and it made me unpopular in some very respectable circles. But here I am wandering again.

[35]James G. Howard came into Los Angeles in 1865, having first practiced law in Sacramento. It was in the Sacramento *Union* that the "Colonel Blove Papers" first appeared. He also wrote an essay on St. Paul which J. J. Ayers called "the production of a mind deeply tinged with profound reverence for sacred subjects, and capable of taking an acute and penetrating insight into the hidden springs of human action." *Gold and Sunshine*, p. 296. During the seventies Howard's home on Main Street was a social and intellectual center and its gardens a landmark. Newmark (pp. 554-555) tells an unhappy story of Howard later using his legal talents for extortion, and Ayers (*Gold and Sunshine*, p. 296) relates the tragic end of the family.

[36]The election occurred on Sept. 5, 1877; Spalding's story appeared in the *Express*, Sept. 8.

Chapter III

THE FIRST REPUBLICAN
NEWSPAPER (1876-1879)[1]

——————————

IN MY MANAGERIAL COGITATIONS one day the thought came to me that Los Angeles ought to be a fair field for a Republican paper. The *Herald* was hard-and-fast Democratic; the *Express* was independent; the *Star* was anything or nothing. In the East the Republican field was undoubtedly the best. In Los Angeles the prevailing sentiment had been Democratic for a long time, and no effort had been made to organize the Republicans, except in time of national elections, and then the movement was rather sporadic. Occasionally in city and county elections there would be a split-off under the title of Independent, or Citizens or Reform ticket, but that meant only a scramble between politicians for the offices. More and more eastern people were sifting in, and the majority of them were Republicans. Why not an evening paper pronouncedly Republican?

I had a confab with Jesse Yarnell, of the Mirror job printing establishment, and gave him my ideas. I knew that Jesse was Republican (back of his fanaticism on temperance); that his establishment was well equipped with type and presses; and it seemed that such an enterprise might appeal to him. But Jesse

[1]Throughout this chapter Spalding assumes the *Evening Republican* (1876-1879) to be the first Republican newspaper in Los Angeles. Actually Jesse Yarnell nearly ten years before had started the Los Angeles *Weekly Republican*, which, however, died after a life of about three years (1867-1870).

turned that sardonic smile of his upon me and said: "I wouldn't be caught dead owning a newspaper." Jesse and his brother had had some experience in helping to found the *Express* a few years previously, and probably that had soured him. I took his emphatic "No" for an answer; but it would be all right for the reader to stick a pin here, for our story will show, a little further on, how Jesse's firm was caught *alive* owning a newspaper.

All prospect for my Republican journal having been reflected in reverse by the Mirror establishment, I took a cue from the fable about the farmer and his grain field and said, "Why not do it myself?" The *Herald* also had a plentiful supply of type, and good press facilities. All that was needed was somebody to start the paper and run it. My friend Creighton had been hanging around the office for a long time, eking out a bare living by such odd jobs as were thrown in his way. He was a competent newspaper man, and had a fair acquaintance with the Los Angeles public; and, besides, he was a Republican.[2] So I put the matter up to Creighton, and he grabbed it. Of course, none of us had any money to invest. But I told Creighton that, if he would start the paper off somehow, and rustle up enough weekly to pay for composition, press-work and paper, we would make no extra charge; and whatever might come from the enterprise was his. And he succeeded in doing that very thing.[3] He was the entire staff—the entire institution. He had no plant and no expense incidental thereto; no office, no rent to pay, no employees. And I never encountered another man who had such a natural capacity for making his headquarters in his hat. He was out cruising about town most of the day, gathering items, drumming up business, making collections; but would drop in at frequent intervals, draw a wad of copy from his pocket, turn it over to the printers, and off again. He did not often sponge table-room even for writing out his notes. He must have prepared his copy as he went along or written it up in any old place that came handy.

It was a marvel how Creighton managed things; but so long as he was on hand every Saturday with his expense bill the rest was no affair of mine. I have an idea that no daily paper was ever run on a lighter basis. The paper was called, on my suggestion, the *Republican*; and it was quite a nice newsy little sheet—no editorials to speak of, but generally some pat and interesting re-

[2]W. W. Creighton was generally active in Republican Party affairs, judging from what Spalding says of him and from the *Express*, July 28, 1877, in which he is reported as acting chairman of the Republican Central Committee.

[3]The first issue appeared Jan. 10, 1876.

prints that served as well; no extensive reports of outstanding events, but a lot of chatter about local happenings.[4]

[The *Republican* started as a four page paper, with the same size of page, the same body-type and general style as the *Herald*; in fact, was manifestly an evening edition of the *Herald*. The chief difference was in size—the *Herald* being eight pages. This made it easy for Creighton, in starting, to borrow a couple of pages, mainly the commercial reports with some advertising (and) the telegraph and reprint matter from the *Herald* forms, which our job foreman took bodily, merely changing the name and page number at the top. That meant half of his paper provided for without the editor turning a hand. Even the service of the foreman in making up was largely gratuitous, for he was on regular salary with the *Herald*, and all Creighton had to do was to tip him moderately and promise more as conditions would naturally improve.

Creighton had secured some advertising patronage in advance, and such ads had already been put in type. That was a start on the remaining two pages, and Creighton must hustle for news, editorial matter and reprint for the remainder. He probably had a drawer full of clippings that would serve on short notice and in hustling up news and editorial comment he was a wizard. He did not depend on taking notes and elaborating afterwards—that was too slow a process. He wrote his item and elaborated his ideas as he went about on his rounds of the village, and as he returned to the office in the course of an hour or two, he carried a pocketful of copy, ready to turn in.

When the time came to close down and go to press, a consultation with the foreman showed how matters stood with the final pages, and if there still was a shortage, why then a little more forceful borrowing. And that was that!

The edition at the start was naturally small, as Creighton had not attempted to obtain subscribers, and all he needed was to provide for street sales and a paper for each of his advertisers, which he would deliver personally. The street venders were only too glad to rally around, take the papers fresh from the press, fold

[4]"The *Evening Republican* . . . was printed at the *Herald* office until the latter part of December, when the *Republican* established an office. In August, 1877, the office was purchased by the Republicans, and the paper published by Allison, Berry & Co. who continued for a few months, when it was conducted by the Republican Printing Co. During most of the time a weekly edition was issued. In Sept., 1878, the daily was discontinued for lack of support, and in Jan., 1879, the weekly also ceased publication." A note from Spalding's papers in possession of Mrs. Helen Groff.

The ensuing six paragraphs in brackets were also written separately by Spalding and are inserted here by the editor.

them and pay the proper stipend to the real editor who was in attendance. These pennies probably constituted the first cash receipts of the new enterprise.

And thus the first Republican newspaper in Los Angeles was launched on less than a shoe-string.

Emerson says that success is built on a foundation of failures. When I note the achievement of the *Times*, which was started a few years after the events which I have just recorded, I feel like congratulating myself on having contributed to one of the failures in its foundation stones. And I am again confirmed in my original opinion that that was a good time to start a Republican paper in Los Angeles!]

The business went on at this rate for several months, until there came a radical change in our establishment; then Creighton transferred his operations to some other printing plant, and I lost track of him.

The scheme might possibly have worked out on its shoe-string if Creighton had not fallen into drinking habits. He was one of those men who could carry quite a lot and not show it. I never saw his face flushed or knew his tongue thickened; I never saw a waver in his walk but once, and that was near the time of his downfall. He was a tall slim man, rather taciturn in speech, and inclined to be sardonic when he expressed himself. He kept on friendly terms with everybody but had no intimate friendships. He never attempted anything brilliant in writing, but could be relied upon for a steady supply of commonplace items. Eventually he disposed of his rights in the *Republican*, and faded out. Soon after my wife and I moved from the little cottage which we had occupied jointly, Creighton married his housekeeper, Emma Drexel. When he dropped out of the picture in Los Angeles, the family may have moved to some other place. The paper was carried on for a year or two longer by Old Man [F. E.] Berry and his son, and a young fellow named Allison. But the Berrys had no capital, and were somewhat erratic themselves, and of such materials great newspapers do not come. But I have thought that, if the little *Republican* had fallen into more stable hands, and had filled the Republican field, and grown with the community, it might have occupied the place that the *Times* subsequently made for itself. But, as the poet has put it,

> Of all sad words of tongue or pen,
> The saddest are these: It might have been.[5]

[5]John Greenleaf Whittier, "Maud Muller."

Local politics were largely dominated those days by a cabal which we called "the Water Company's ring." It was organized along the old lines of ward and convention manipulation which eventually made the system so odious that it was discarded entirely. Ed Niles was the local boss. He was a young fellow of fine natural endowment, pleasant address, good education and great shrewdness. He had no visible means of support, other than politics, unless it were certain connections in the lower part of town that were regarded as very compromising. Barney Fehnemann was his trusted lieutenant.[6] The party management, as embodied in the central committee, was always under control of the ring. When ward conventions were called to select delegates to a convention, there were enough subservient creatures of the cabal to stock it, and their prepared slate went through. Then as now, a great many of the best people thought it not worth while, or infra dig, to dabble in preliminary politics. Hence, Niles made up the ward slates; Niles stocked the conventions; Niles virtually put up the ticket that the Water Company selected, and then the people were graciously allowed to vote for it. There was no recourse unless a lot of kickers got together and nominated an opposition ticket, which at best was apt to be a forlorn hope.

Before I had yet made myself obnoxious to the gang, Niles met me on the street one day, just before convention time, and casually asked if I would like to go as a delegate. I acquiesced, he made a memorandum on a slip of paper, and the next heard of the matter was that I had been duly elected. I must have proven recalcitrant in convention, and in fact there developed quite a little band of recalcitrants who refused to vote for the slate. We made quite a ruction, but of course could not upset the well-laid plan. Niles never again gave me an invitation. In fact, when I went to the polls to cast my ballot, I found Niles installed as judge of election, with several young men for assistants whom I spotted as recruits from the under world. Niles took my ticket, and placidly threw it under the table. Such manifest and brazen abuses in time created a good deal of indignation in the community. By the time the next election came round, there was an organized movement of the younger men, who wanted something better.

[6]During the hard times in Los Angeles following the collapse of the boom, Barney Fehnemann established in 1889 a free labor exchange for the unemployed. It attracted wide attention, and a similar exchange in San Francisco was patterned upon it; but when the city council denied support, it disintegrated. Grace Heilman Stimson, *Rise of the Labor Movement in Los Angeles* (Berkeley, 1955), p. 94.

The Second Ward comprised that portion of the city lying west of Main Street and north of Temple, taking in just a little fringe of Sonoratown.[7] The voters were nearly all Americans. It was in this ward that the movement started. When the primary was called we were somewhat astonished to find that the polling-place was in an adobe building in Sonoratown. Ed Niles was judge, as usual. Our organization met at headquarters and marched to the polls together early in the morning. We had previously obtained from the central committee an order that one of our members should be admitted to the booth as a watcher. When we drew up to the polls and presented our credentials, Niles refused to comply. Without further to-do we grabbed our representative, Cap. Hutton, by the legs and hoisted him in through the window. Cap was a burly fellow, weighing nearly two hundred pounds, and built like a prize-fighter.[8] If a scrap had been started, he was competent and willing to clean out the whole crowd of inferiors that constituted Niles's support. And if he had needed assistance he could have got it in a minute or two. But no scrap was started. Our representative staid through the day, and saw that the voters of the ward got a square deal. The rest of us remained about the polls, saw that Cap was fairly treated, and did politics. And the outcome was that the Second Ward sent its own delegation to the convention. I wish that the full list of those early, practical reformers could be given; those whom I remember were Cap. Hutton, Frank A. Gibson, Fred Wood, Dr. Le Moyne Wills, and E. T. Wright.[9] They were all residents of the Second Ward. How much of an impression our delegation

[7]Sonoratown was the Mexican quarter of the city, just north of the Plaza, notorious for saloons and fights. In the city at the time there were four wards, each represented in the city council.

[8]There is a remote possibility that this was Aurelius W. Hutton, who had served in the Civil War and hence might have been called "Cap." But, if so, it is strange that Spalding does not mention his profession of attorney, especially since Aurelius Hutton appears in Spalding's *History*, II, 65.

[9]Francis Asbury Gibson came to Los Angeles in 1872. With Fred Wood and some others he founded the firm which later became the Title Insurance and Trust Company. Gibson and Spalding were to be associated for many years in such organizations as the Unitarian Church, the Los Angeles Athletic Club, and the Sunset Club.

William Le Moyne Wills later became one of the city's leading physicians. In 1887 he was instrumental in bringing the first crematory west of the Rockies to Los Angeles (Newmark, p. 567). He was on the Board of Education from 1892 to 1896.

Edward Thomas Wright came to Los Angeles in 1875 because of a heart condition, which, however, did not deter his activity as engineer and surveyor. He was elected county surveyor in 1882, 1884, and 1895. He surveyed for subdividers like H. K. S. O'Melveny and I. W. Hellman, for the Cajon Ditch to Anaheim, and for numerous Pacific Electric Railway rights of way. Spalding, *History*, II, 353-355.

made on the convention I cannot recall, but at any rate, a departure had been made, an example had been set, of what a few determined voters could do if they only set themselves at it with sufficient determination. And as time went on the reform movement grew and grew. We had liberated the Geni from the bottle.

There was an incident in one of our early conventions in Turner Hall that I have often recalled with a chuckle. A fellow named Carpenter was holding the convention with a long-winded speech and everybody was dead tired of him. The subject seemed to be as dry for the speaker as for his auditors, as with the conclusion of every second sentence, he would turn to the table and take a drink of water. Finally Louie Thorne, one of the delegates, stood up in his place, and said:

"Mr. Speaker, I arise to a point of order."

"State your point," said the chairman.

"I object, Sir, to a man running a wind-mill on water power."

The convention was in a roar of laughter, which delayed the speaker a minute or so; and after he had got started again, the joke got its second wind and broke out more heartily than before. After that he did not try more than two or three times, and as the situation grew funnier every minute, he was finally compelled to subside.[10]

Those old conventions were a queer combination, take them altogether. With a bar in front of the building, inviting first and last calls, and a door opening directly into the convention hall, it is manifest that liquidation was one of the important functions of the gathering. Yet it was not common to see a drunken man on the floor of the convention, and if a delegate had shown that he was obstreperously under the influence his friends would have hustled him out. It was not unusual, however, to find a country delegate or two snugly tucked away in a corner of the bar sound asleep.

[10]The only Carpenter listed in the directory of 1875 is F. J. Carpenter of the police department. Francis J. Carpenter was city jailer in 1855-1857 and 1859-1861; also election inspector, 1859-1860. Spalding in his *History*, I, 196, refers to a Frank Carpenter who owned a wooden shack on First Street which the city rented for the *zanjero*.

Chapter IV

OLD TIME JOURNALISM
(1874-1878)

L os Angeles was a dull town. Of course the routine reports
did not stir up much interest; there was little doing in
crime of a sensational sort; very few shows to report; no society events that called for elaboration, and if we had had a real
juicy divorce case, I doubt if we would have known what to do
with it. Probably it would have been tried behind closed doors,
as *contra bones mores*, and the newspapers would not have tried
to pry into it. I sometimes think it would be better if we had
things that way now.

Impressed with the general atmosphere of dullness, I put forth
my best endeavors to stir up something different. We published
only six days in the week—no Monday paper. That gave us Sunday free, and I frequently improved the opportunity to make a
trip into the country, if somebody invited me to ride in his buggy,
or I made short excursions into the suburbs on foot. Perhaps a
little jaunt down Alameda Street, through the small farms, or a
trip out Main Street as far as Washington, would furnish material for a rather flamboyant article in Tuesday's paper on the
beauties of nature in general, and the wonderful productiveness
and many attractions of Southern California. My old scrap-book
shows an assortment of articles with headings such as,[1]

[1]The following three articles, representative passages of which are inserted by
the editor, were printed in the *Herald* in this order: May 26, May 6, and May 19,

OUT OF TOWN.

A Sunday's Jaunt to the Country on Foot—Some Self-complaciencies
in Regard to Our Country and Climate—Mr. A. F. Waterman's Place
on San Pedro Street.

[Our path lay out San Pedro street, and we jogged along in the comfortable frame of mind usually attributed to the poor but honest man.
About two miles and a half from town our walk terminated at the
house of our hospitable friend, A. F. Waterman. San Pedro street is too
well known to require any words of description from us. Suffice it that
we followed along the cool zanja, passed the old Dutchman's place and
thoroughly appreciated all the beauties of field, grove and garden
spread out along the way. Mr. Waterman lives upon a small place
containing about six acres of land, with a cosy little cottage house and
the other conveniences which your Eastern bred man is sure to have
around him. This place, however, is only rented, and Mr. Waterman
has his farm proper about a mile and a half further on, where, in company with Mr. Thompson, he owns a ranch of one hundred and thirteen acres. On the homestead property Mr. Waterman has a small
nursery, which will be a fortune in itself before many years. He has
a large number of seedling forest trees, brought from Wisconsin,
Michigan, Ohio and New York, of which he makes a specialty. They
consist of ash, beech, American chestnut and several varieties of maple.
They have been brought here at great expense and trouble, and will
require a world of care still before they become large enough to take
care of themselves. With very few exceptions, they are doing finely.
They will be ready to transplant by the coming of next Winter, and
will then bring about fifty cents each. For some of the varieties Mr.
Waterman has double and treble the number of orders that he will be
able to fill. These same trees are sold as high as a dollar and a half
apiece in San Francisco. Much credit is due Mr. Waterman for the
efforts which he is making to introduce these new varieties of trees
into our country; it is by the enterprise of such men that the land is
brought out to its fullest capacity of production and that we are shown
what really can be done here. . . .

After making an examination of the ranch to our thorough satisfas-
tion, we again returned to Mr. Waterman's house, where we partook
of the hospitalities of his board with a gusto bred of our long walk.
Not to extend our regards to Mr. Waterman's estimable wife, would be
an ill-deserved slight; neither can we pass over her Yankee-made
strawberry short-cake in silence. It was a triumph of the cuisine art;

1874. Other articles in which Spalding does similar "rambling" were in the *Herald*,
Feb. 19, 1876 (to the end of the Southern Pacific Railroad construction in the San
Gorgonio Pass), and the *Express*, Dec. 8, 1877 (to the west of town).

Excerpts from Spalding's newspaper stories when added by the editor are both here
and in all subsequent cases reproduced without correcting typographical errors. Such
additions have been bracketed here and throughout; footnotes will distinguish this
kind of material from bracketed editorial comment.

and the way the Judge and the General stowed it away made our reportorial cheeks crimson for very shame. But there is an end to all things, even to strawberry short-cakes and Sunday pasears. Thus we chronicle the events of another pleasant day, and return thanks to our friends out of town.]

A FLYING TRIP TO SAN FERNANDO.

Glorious Day, Picturesque Scenery, Lovely Valleys and a Promising Town—A Gratuitous Prescription for the "Mollygrubs."

[When Sunday comes around, and you are well worn out with the business cares of the week; with an ache in the head and a creak in the back, and you get up in the morning saying "demmit," here is a pannacea for your malady: the train for San Fernando starts at 11:30 A.M. Take your crotchety self off to the depot at that time, and if your better fraction (provided you are fortunate enough to have one) and the youngters take a fancy to accompany you, let them go along. At all events, go to San Fernando; it will do you a trifle more good than the best sermon known to theology. . . . After the sandy, desert-like stretch, we again reach the fertile plain, and here is San Fernando. The trip of twenty-one miles has been made in an hour, although it hardly seems a lapse of ten minutes. Considering the fact that the town is not yet a month old, San Fernando presents an uncommonly lively appearance. A commodious depot has been built, and this is already well filled; a portion being used for offices and passenger rooms, and the warehouse well filled with goods for transit. There is also a boarding house and bar, well patronized, of course—especially the latter (as yet they have no water to speak of in San Fernando); and several other buildings are rapidly assuming shape.

The Telegraph Stage Line now makes its headquarters here, and is building stables and corral. Mr. W. P. Reynolds, with his surveying party, has his tent pitched on the bank of the creek south of the town site.]

UP THE MOUNTAINS.

Our New Mining Discoveries—What There is of Them and What They Promise—A Trip to the Mountains North of Los Angeles and What We Saw by the Way.

[Quietly and persistently, for a year or more past, Mr. J. A. Bell has been prospecting through the range of mountains lying north of our city. Something over a week ago he found a lead which struck him as being more than usually promising; he secured specimens, had them assayed, and his impressions were confirmed. Then, without sounding a trumpet before him, or attempting a display of his good fortune, he entered his claims, made his discoveries known to a few of our leading citizens, formed a company for working the lead, and there, as the legal term goes, "rests his case."

[48]

A few days ago our reporter received an invitation to visit the new claims, and in company with two well known citizens made the trip by way of a Sunday pasear. There was no intention to break the Sabbath, but the day was so charming, the air so clear, and the mountains and valleys so inviting, that the temptation was too great to be resisted, and we simply suspended the fourth commandment and went.]

And so forth, and so forth, and so forth. It was good exercise for the young reporter, and it didn't do the readers of the *Herald* any harm. Maybe some of them read it.

Then I furthered acquaintance with every man from the country whom I met, and by giving him a nice personal mention, and sending him a marked copy of the paper, got him into the notion of coming to the office and calling for me and giving all the recent happenings in his neighborhood, the state of the crops, and so on. I also cultivated sea-faring men who drifted up from Wilmington, and got news and incidents and sea yarns—anything that would make a story. I looked up some of the old Dons, like Don Juan Warner, Don Mateo Keller, Don Stephen C. Foster, Don Antonio Coronel, Don Pedro Carrillo—all of the old-timers were Dons in those days—and got from them interesting bits of history and tradition and romance concerning the town and the long past Spanish-Mexican era. That this mine held many pay streaks is attested by my old scrap-book, from which I gather, scattered along, such heads as the following:

The Desert Phantom.

Fort Hill. Another Chapter in Its History.

Euchered on a Lone Hand. A Pioneer Sketch.

Medicine; This Side Up.

Whistle or Burn.

Senorita Francisca. A Romance of Los Angeles County.

A Cool Desperado, And How he Met His Fate—An Episode in the History of Los Angeles. [The lynching of Lachenais, 1870].

A Frenzied Raid—How Nineteen Chinamen were Executed, Without Benefit of Clergy, in 1871.[2]

[2]Spalding's collection of scrapbooks is in the Huntington Library (California Scrapbook 41, 13 vols.) and will hereafter be cited as Scrapbook 1-13.

All of the above stories except the last are in Scrapbook 1. "The Desert Phantom" was "Written for the Sunday Chronicle" (presumably of San Francisco) and is signed Mary D. Spalding, Los Angeles! Spalding has dated it by hand Jan. 14, 1878. "Fort Hill: Another Chapter" is neither signed nor dated (but a story titled only "Fort Hill" was in the *Herald*, Nov. 14, 1874). The next four appeared under the name Adolphus Perkins, and no date is noted in the scrapbook. "A Cool Desperado" appeared in the *Express*, Aug. 13, 1877.

One yarn, that Don Mateo Keller spun for me, I told as nearly as possible in his own words, and it appeared under the following head:

THE BURIED TREASURE.

A Legend of the Early days of Los Angeles—Fifty thousand dollars of old Don Tiburcio Tapia's money which lies concealed in the Arroyo Seco—Interesting reminiscence of thirty years ago.[3]

"There were," it seems, "two wooden boxes," iron bound, "it may be the width of a span and twice as long and deep," and they were "filled with Spanish doubloons, each piece weighing an ounce and valued at sixteen dollars." And all this was buried, with circumstantial description, in the sands of the Arroyo Seco; and Don Tiburcio had died, and his son Ramon had come back, and traced out the chart that the old man left, and had found the cross with one arm pointing to the spot, and had dug and dug, but never could find the treasure. Oh, it was a dandy, and it traveled all over the country. We used to get letters about it a year afterwards. One dear old lady wrote that she had dreamed the place where the doubloons were buried, and if somebody would pay her fare to California, she would go right to it, and divide the proceeds. Another correspondent had seen the article in the New York *Sun*, and having been in California himself in an early day, he felt tolerably sure that he could locate the boxes. He, also, was willing to divide.

[*To the Editor of the Herald:*

Sir: I have seen in to-day's New York *Sun*, newspaper, an account of hidden treasure. I am a laboring man. I have been in California. I went there after the war. I worked at Santa Cruz on the railroad for a few months. There were then a good many emigrants to Los Angeles to settle on Governor Downey's land in Lower California. I wanted my comrade to come down by land or water, but he backed out and would not go with me, so I returned to the States. Now, Sir, while I was working at Santa Cruz for a fuse factory, in the employ of a man by the name of Lynch, I dreamed a dream of such treasure. In my dream, the box was iron, the money was doubloons, and some smaller pieces of coin. This account sprung my old dream. Now, Mr. Editor, if there is any truth in dreams, I saw the old man Tiburcio Tapia. If this man Raman is his genuine son, I would go to California and find the treasure for him if he would pay my way there and back to New

---

[3]The story is in Spalding's Scrapbook 1 and dated by hand March 1876. A second article, "That Buried Treasure," from which the subsequent letter is quoted, was in the *Herald*, April 27, 1876. A rewrite of the episode appeared in the *Express* during Spalding's tenure, Dec. 6, 1877.

York in case of failure. In case it came out right I claim one-half, and will pay my own way back to New York. Mr. Editor, please give this note full consideration before you consign it to the waste basket. I remain your obedient servant,

James Brady.

Direct your letter to Flat Bush Postoffice, Long Island, State of New York, in care of John Brady, Milkman. J.B.]

On a tip from one of my sea-faring friends, I slipped down to Wilmington, and found a party of Gilbert Islanders who had been rescued at sea and brought in by a sailing ship from Australia. They had gone out in a catamaran, had been blown beyond their reckoning by a storm, had cruised helplessly around for several days, and were nearly famished when picked up. I found the party in the back room of a saloon where the Good Samaritan of a barkeeper had given them shelter. The women were in calico dresses, and the men wore a choice assortment of sailor clothes that had been donated. There were several children. Both men and women were smoking cob pipes when I arrived, but they soon laid them aside at the call for dinner. The meal was abundantly spread on a round table, and when they had been seated properly, they all bowed their heads while the leader said grace in the native tongue. I got the complete story, with all the high-lights that the sailor-folk could throw into it—the Islanders couldn't speak English. And it was a scoop! Now, do you mind that? A clear scoop!

One of my maritime friends was Captain Janes, who had anchored just above tide-water at San Pedro, near Timms's Point.[4] He had a wife somewhat larger than himself, and more formidable. The Captain had built a little shack out of driftwood, and had made some simple homelike furniture. The pair subsisted at first mainly on clams and mussels, which were easily obtainable on the beach, and made very good eating, if you did not have to take them for a steady diet. The Captain had enough capital, I think, to buy a wheelbarrow—maybe he borrowed it—and with that he set up in business. That business was the furnishing of sand ballast to empty out-going sailing craft. The sand, of course,

[4]John F. Janes was a colorful filibusterer, once described as "ex-sailor, ex-miner, ex-explorer, and ex-ward politician." After 1883 he sporadically published the San Pedro *Shipping Gazette* in which he fumed against monopoly (especially the Southern Pacific Railroad), against Phineas Banning, and against the Chinese. Stimson, *Labor Movement*, p. 62, feels that Janes was one of the leaders of anti-Chinese feeling during the 1880's in southern California, and without his blustering presence Los Angeles would not have preceded San Francisco in such agitation.

cost him nothing, and all he had to do was to wheel it aboard and dump it in the hold, and he got good money for it. By and by he developed a spring in the hills back of his shack, and then he enlarged the scope of his business, furnishing to ships ballast *and* water. As the Captain was an old sea dog himself, and good-natured, energetic, prompt and reliable, he soon worked into the good graces of many of the masters of the smaller craft, and prospered accordingly. I think, also, his prices were reasonable, since he did not have to hire any help, and made no claim to a monopoly. So wide-awake was he to his opportunities, that he finally built a flatboat that served for a lighter, and that helped mightily. Then he added another lighter or two. But, while his business was thus growing by leaps and bounds, so to speak, and he had been able to establish a status at the grocery store, and he and his wife no longer ate clams and mussels, except as luxuries now and then —while this was going on, he was infringing upon the vested rights of the Wilmington Transportation Company, which everybody but Captain Janes knew had a mortal cinch on all that kind of maritime business.[5] One evil night a gang of Wilmington toughs made a descent on the San Pedro beach, and scuttled and sank the Captain's lighters. It was at this juncture that Captain Janes made a trip to Los Angeles, and poured his tale of woe into my ear. It appealed to me as a good newspaper story, and that the Captain really had some show of right and justice on his side. So I published a full account of the affair.

The Commodore of the Wilmington Transportation Company called at our office the next day and made my acquaintance. He was a large, affable gentleman, and was not ill-tempered at all; on the contrary, he put his arm around me in a fatherly way, and advised me not to give any credence to those people down at the point; they were a disreputable set. As for Janes, he was a regular vagabond, and his wife, oh, my! In response to my questioning, the Commodore admitted that some hard characters of Wilmington had scuttled the Captain's lighters, but it was a mere frolic, and probably they were drunk. "Don't get mixed up in their rows down there," he advised. "It won't do you or your paper any good; they're a hard lot. And, you know, I take the *Herald* myself, and think a whole lot of it; in fact, it is my favor-

[5]The Wilmington Transportation Company was formed about 1877 by Phineas Banning after the Central Pacific Railroad abandoned Santa Monica for San Pedro as a port for Los Angeles and, in response to criticisms of monopoly, sold its lighterage equipment to Banning. Maymie Krythe, *Port Admiral: Phineas Banning, 1830-1885* (San Francisco, 1957), pp. 213-214.

ite paper—or always has been until that foolish article of yours appeared the other day."

Then, if my memory is reliable, I went over to Roger's Palace and had a drink with the Admiral—no, I mean the Commodore.[6]

But Captain Janes kept me advised from day to day of the state of things down at the point, and I kept the public advised. In time the Captain managed to fish up his lighters, and repair them, and the opposition business went on. Captain Janes remained my fast friend for years, and many a good sea-story did he throw into my hands. One day, in a burst of good feeling he said, "Why don't you go down and get hold of a piece of ground at the point? I tell you San Pedro is going to be the port, some day, and all that land, that can be had for a song now, is going to be valuable." But I knew the Captain to be rather erratic and visionary, and didn't take any stock in his prophecies. And besides, I hadn't any money to invest about that time. It was a case of Chicago and the pair of boots.

I was undoubtedly indebted to Capt. Janes, directly or indirectly, for the following marine yarns or inventions:[7]

SEAL HUNTING.

A Three Months' Cruise in the Isabella W. among the Islands off Our Coast—Incidents and Accidents of the Trip, as Gathered from One of the Crew.

[A few days since we had a call from Messrs. Miller and Daly, two fair representatives of the "joliy tar"—genial, whole-souled men, by the way—who have just returned from a seal hunting trip among some of the small islands of the Pacific. . . .

On the 13th of January last, the Isabella W. put out from Santa Cruz, well provisioned and armed for a war upon the innocents. The schooner was furnished and equipped by Captain Timms of San Pedro, and Miller and Daly, accompanied by a Mexican boy as cook and general roust-about, made up the party in charge. About 1,600 seal were taken, which furnished a yield of 3,500 gallons of oil. . . . The young seals were mostly shot while cavorting around in the water near the shore. About 2,500 Henry rifle cartridges were thus shot away, and in every five

[6]The "Commodore" probably refers to Phineas Banning, who was, however, at this time usually designated "General." His son William managed the Wilmington Transportation Company during Phineas' frequent absences, but the younger man, born in 1858, does not seem to fit Spalding's picture. There is another possibility. Janes in the *Shipping Gazette*, Nov. 17, 1883, tells of "Capt. Polhemus, Gen. Banning's Commodore." (The name is Albert A. Polhamus in the *Great Register of Los Angeles County* [Los Angeles, 1879].) In the context none of these seems as likely as Phineas himself.

[7]"Seal Hunting," *Herald*, May 7, 1874; "Earning a Ship," *Express*, Jan. 16, 1878.

shots three or four of the festive creatures were called upon to deliver up the ghost and join the cremating society. . . .

The Isabella starts on another sealing expedition in a few days, this time going after "bull seals"; and she will be out until about the Fourth of July. . . . Our friend Miller has promised to furnish us some more points concerning this coming trip, and in due time the readers of the HERALD will dream of the maneuvres of the Isabella W. ". . . Here's to a lucky voyage and a safe return!"]

EARNING A SHIP.
How a Stylish and Well Educated Young Gentleman of Philadelphia went to Sea for a Term of Two Years Before the Mast.

The latter story was not that of Dana revamped, as one might think, at first glance, but of a young man named Lord. Captain Janes was an active fellow intellectually as well as physically, and being located at the point, where smaller ships were bound to pass in entering the channel, and nearest the anchorage of larger vessels that stopped in the offing, and being hail fellow with the sailors, and on speaking terms with the lesser officers, he was invaluable in giving early information of marine news, as well as conveying some things that did not sift through in an official way. I could well afford to throw the Admiral overboard for a real sailor like Capt. Janes.

In cruising about for matters of interest, I ran across an old winery, in the edge of Sonoratown, just above the plaza—Pelanconi's—and that struck me as a good subject. So, in the wine making season, I visited the place and wrote up the process. Perhaps, now that wine-making, particularly of that sort, and wine of all sorts are virtually obsolete, a brief quotation from that article of long ago may have some historical interest.[8]

Substantially the same system of manufacture is pursued in some of our establishments as that in vogue among the Jews two thousand years ago. At Pelanconi's place may be marked a close analogy to the ancient system. . . . The grapes fresh from the vineyard are dumped into a large vat provided with a double, or false bottom, the upper one consisting of open slats, which allow the crushed mass of pulp to pass through to the lower receptacle, while the stems and coarser refuse remain on top. Into these large boxes, when filled with the luscious grapes, a half dozen swarthy natives step with bare feet and legs, and perform the process of

[8]The directory of 1875 twice spells the name Antonio Palanconi, manufacturer of wines on Alameda Street opposite the Sisters of Charity School. Spalding's account here freely edits the newspaper story (*Herald*, probably early 1877), a clipping of which is in his Scrapbook 1.

"treading." A recent local writer, describing this procedure, went into details concerning the motley group, as they tread and sweat, and sweat and tread, while the rich juice and pulp oozed up between their toes. Perhaps it is well to avoid too much minuteness in describing this method of wine-making. Some people would fail to see the poetry in it, and some with squeamish stomachs might not relish their dinner glass of claret for knowing that, in its primitive state, it had gushed between the nut-brown toes of a native. But, if they are captious at this stage of the proceeding, what will they say when we describe another ancient feature? We have stated that, after undergoing the treading process, the must is removed to the fermenting tubs; here it is allowed to remain for twelve, fifteen or eighteen days, the period depending upon the temperature of the weather. Some of the tubs in the more advanced state of fermentation showed their contents raised high in a frothy mass over the top rim, while the juice trickled down the outside, looking much like violet-tinted soap-suds. (Excuse the comparison.)

In one of the tubs we saw a man carrying out the further process alluded to. He had nothing about him particularly dressy, except a woolen shirt. His brawny legs sank into the mass of pulp, down, down, down—well, until the skirts of the aforementioned garment were thoroughly draggled in the rich juice. He would undoubtedly have sunk out of sight, but a decent regard for appearances and his love of life induced him to cling tenaciously to a large pole laid across the top of the vat. This, as we have said, is another ancient custom. It is recorded by Latin writers that, while the mass was fermenting, a naked man entered the *dolia*, or casks, and, by agitating the mass, kept it from souring, while the warmth of his body imparted to it peculiar virtues, and assisted fermentation.

We charged Mr. Pelanconi nothing for that write-up, and maybe Mr. Pelanconi thought it wasn't worth anything. But shucks! It was *el costumbre del pais*—the way it always had been done in California, and nobody thought anything about it—they preferred not to think, which was also an old Spanish custom.

A friend of mine who had the entrée of a Spanish family at a hacienda—a country home, a few miles out San Pedro Street— got me an invitation, and one Sunday I accompanied him, to make a call and enjoy a real Spanish dinner. The fact that there were two very attractive señoritas in the family may have had some bearing. We were very pleasantly received, and although the Don and his Doña did not speak English, the young ladies did, and altogether we were made to feel at home.

Everything was new and strange to me in the great rambling adobe house, and I was on the *qui-vive* for fresh experiences. Dinner was served in an ample apartment, the cook-stove within easy reach. The table was of plain boards, innocent of cloth or any other fol-de-rol, but it was abundantly stocked with attractive comestibles. We sat on long wooden benches drawn up on each side, and the Doña busied herself in cooking tortillas—immense pancakes of a brownish color, which, as they matured, were doubled over and passed around in the Doña's deft hand. Each person at table tore off a piece suited to his requirement, and the good work went on. An abundance of red wine was on the table, a quart bottle at each plate. There were platters filled with delicious looking viands, the name of each being told as we were helped. I cannot recall them entirely, but remember the *frijoles con caiso*, red beans garnished with cheese, which were delicious. Another dish, of a bright red color, they called *chile con carne*, and I noticed just the faintest shade of a smile as they mentioned it. Now there is a bit of subtle Castilian humor in this name. If you say *carne con chile*—meat with pepper—that is one thing; if you say *chile con carne*—pepper with meat—that is another. In the latter instance, pepper—and red pepper at that—is the chief factor, the principal ingredient, the *chef d'oeuvre*, so to speak, and the meat is a mere negligible item. All this I found out afterward, when it was too late to do any good. Without premonition of any sort, I got a mouthful of the stuff, and it was all red pepper—no *con* and no *carne* in it; all ch———. No, I cannot use the word; it is a part of that grim Castilian humor. Yes, I swallowed it. I would probably have done so had it been live coals, rather than make a sputter, and get myself laughed at. But there were tears in my eyes—not of grief, but anguish. Just anguish! After that I partook of nothing red but the wine, which seemed to have a cooling effect all the way down. The *frijoles* and the *tortillas* I ate of sparingly, for while innocent in themselves, they seemed to add fuel to the flames. The red wine was my chief stand-by, and I was thankful that there was a whole bottle of it right at hand to keep down the conflagration.

One day news sifted in through the Sheriff's office that there had been a murder out at El Monte. I secured a horse and buggy at the livery stable, and a man who knew the country to drive, and went out to gather the particulars first hand. A man named Gibson had been killed in a neighborhood fracas. It seemed to me quite an expedition, and a real up-to-date stroke of newspaper enterprise.[9]

[9]A story in the *Herald*, June 6, 1874, conforms to this description in all respects, except that the victim's name was W. T. Turner and that he was badly wounded but not killed.

One of the most sensational episodes of those early times was the robbery of old man Repetto, an Italian sheep owner, whose ranch was in the Puente hills, north of the present town of Fullerton. Repetto was a massive old fellow, weighing about three hundred pounds, and was reputed to be wealthy. The robbery was perpetrated by [Tiburcio] Vasquez and his gang, who had recently transferred their field of outlawry from one of the northern counties, where it started, and had established a safe retreat somewhere in the Verdugo mountains. This robbery occurred in the spring of 1874, and must have been shortly before my arrival in Los Angeles.[10]

I have already given some description of the old adobe city building on Spring Street, and the chamber in which the Council held its sessions. One Thursday afternoon in April, 1874, while that august body was in the midst of its laborious duties, and everything "as quiet as a painted ship upon a painted ocean," a crowd surged up around the door, and somebody shouted, "Vasquez is caught." Without awaiting the formality of an adjournment, the council dissolved, the members individually jumping over the railing and running out of the door. I had to stop a moment to gather up my papers, and that was well, for it gave me a chance at a second thought. That was to the effect that it would do no good to go the same way the councilmen had gone, for I would simply be caught in the jam and couldn't get anywhere. So I went to the rear window which, as before remarked, was only about two feet square, and opening it, I crawled through into the jail yard. I found the Jailer just opening his wicket door, and in an instant the officers came in, carrying Vasquez, who had been wounded. They carried him to the little jail in the middle of the lot, and laid him on the floor of the entrance-way, or lobby. That was the best receiving hospital Los Angeles afforded. The crowd in the street were strictly barred out, and only the Sheriff's posse admitted. In a few moments the wicket door was again opened to admit Dr. K[enneth] D. Wise, a surgeon [and city health officer], who had been summoned. The wounded bandit had already been relieved of most of his clothing, and Dr. Wise, without bothering about anaesthetics, proceeded in workmanlike fashion to cut out the buckshot which had lodged in the man's arms and legs, and were just beneath the skin. As I remember it, Vasquez winced a little under the operation, but he made no outcry, and

[10]Spalding here inserted from Newmark (p. 454) the account of the Alessandro Repetto robbery and Vasquez' theft of Charlie Miles's watch. Since it is readily available elsewhere, it is omitted in this edition.

[57]

maintained a rather jovial, bantering air through it all. Dr. J. P. Widney was next admitted to the jail yard, but the extraction of buckshot had been concluded by that time.[11] Meanwhile I was busy, getting from members of the Sheriff's party a full and circumstantial account of the capture. Shortly the wicket door again swung, and Charlie Miles came in. He and Vasquez hailed each other like old cronies, talking in Spanish, and I expect Charlie was really glad to see him, under the circumstances. Vasquez called for his vest, and handed back the gold watch of which he had so adroitly secured the loan in the Arroyo Seco a short time before. Charlie asked about the chain, and Vasquez had that fished out from another article of clothing.

Probably my account of the capture of Vasquez, written when the facts were fresh in mind, and with the unusually good opportunity I enjoyed for gathering the particulars from authentic sources, would be worth producing as a matter of history. I am aware that a modern, up-to-date reporter would make much more of such an exciting episode; giving a separate interview with each member of the capturing party, the Sheriff's story, the prisoner's story, his picture, the pictures of all concerned, a picture of Greek George's house (perhaps faked), the record of Greek George, a comprehensive history of Vasquez's career, the pedigree of each member of his band, and pictures of any able-bodied Mexicans available. But there would be about half a dozen modern reporters and a staff of artists, set to work on these various details, and after all, they would not get many more of the essential, compressed facts, and might not get them so accurately as I did, and they would give the same essential narrative a dozen times over. I insist that, in some respects, the old way was better; its compilation was less expensive and it was at least a time-saver for readers.[12]

Vasquez has been pictured by latter-day romancers as a veritable *caballero*, a magnificent, commanding specimen of human-

[11]Dr. Joseph P. Widney was later involved with his brother, Robert M. Widney, in the founding of a Methodist college, which became the University of Southern California. Dr. Widney was the first dean of its medical school (1885).

[12]Spalding forgets that for at least a month before the capture the papers had been full of Vasquez and that his own story in the *Herald*, May 15, 1874, was followed the next day by an even longer interview with the bandit by the *Herald*'s editor, which covered a good number of the aspects that he attributes to more modern reporting. Spalding's own report on the capture is reprinted in its entirety in his *History*, I, 213-216. An additional interview with Vasquez is reprinted from the *Star*, May 16, 1874, in Robert G. Cleland's *The Cattle on a Thousand Hills* (San Marino, Calif., 1951), pp. 274-279.

ity, and all that. One of them, recently presenting such a description, called him "Velasquez," getting the name mixed with that of a celebrated Spanish painter. Vasquez was not that sort of an Indian, for Indian he was, and small Indian at that. Not over five feet four or five inches in height, weight about a hundred and forty pounds, lithe and muscular as a catamount, with a keen eye, swart complexion, straight black hair, straggling mustache and whiskers—he was anything but a commanding figure, and appeared just what he was, a low-down, brutal Sonoranian "greaser." After remaining in the Los Angeles jail for a month or so, during which he recovered from his wounds and received no end of flowers and tender messages from admiring women, he was taken up to Santa Clara county, where he was tried and convicted of murder, and was duly hanged.

This history would be incomplete if I should fail to tell about Don Mateo Keller and his El Dorado wine. He was not a real Don, any more than were lots of others who enjoyed that title by courtesy, and his given name was not Mateo, but Matthew. He was an Irishman, born on the ould sod, and he had enough of the Irish twirl in his talk to make it very delicious. Educated for a Catholic priest originally, he had broken away from his moorings, and drifted out to this strange, far-away wilderness while still a young man, settling in Los Angeles in 1856. Here he acquired land, planted him a vineyard, and accumulated much goods. All that part of town from the corner of Los Angeles and Aliso streets north and east to the river belonged to him, and his vineyard was where our old Chinatown is located. His winery, a large, rambling brick building fronting on Alameda Street, was his headquarters when I knew him, but at an earlier day he had also conducted a business on Los Angeles Street.[13] Mr. Harris Newmark has this reference to him:

Matthew Keller, or Don Mateo, as he was called, . . . was a quaint personality of real ability, who had a shop on the northwest corner of Los Angeles and Commercial streets, and owned the adjoining store in which P. Beaudry had been in business. His operations were original and his advertising unique, as will be seen from his announcement in the *Star* in February [1861]: . . .

[13]According to his grandson, John M. Keller of Larkspur, Calif., and according to the *Herald* of Jan. 7, 1875, Matthew Keller came to Los Angeles in 1851, five years earlier than Spalding indicated. By Spalding's time, in the middle 1870's, Keller's 100,000 vines were only exceeded in the Los Angeles basin by growers like B. D. Wilson and L. J. Rose. Keller served on the city council, 1852-1853 and 1868-1869. For his ownership of the Malibu Rancho, see William W. Robinson, *The Malibu* (Los Angeles, 1958).

"M. Keller, to His Customers
The Right of Secession Admitted!

You are hereby notified that the time has arrived when you must pay up, without further delay, or I shall be obliged to invoke the aid of the law and the lawyers.

After such settlement, slow-payers are requested to secede.

M. Keller.

(to be augmented next week)"

This advertisement, Mr. Newmark says, parenthesis and all, continued in the *Star*, week after week, for at least twelve months.

The following year, Keller, in flaring headlines, offered for sale the front of his Los Angeles vineyard, facing on Aliso Street, in building lots of twenty by one hundred feet, saying, in his prospectus:

"Great improvements are on the *tapis* in this quarter. Governor Downey and the intrepid Beaudry propose to open a street to let the light of day shine in upon their dark domains. On the Equerry side of Aliso Street, 'what fine legs your master has,' must run to give way for more permanent fixtures. Further on, the Prior estates are about to be improved by the astute and far-seeing Templito; and Keller sells lots on the sunny side of Aliso Street. The map is on view at my office; come in and make your selections,—first come, first served! Terms will be made handy!

M. Keller."[14]

Don Mateo certainly had a rare gift of language, a vocabulary that was full and voluptuous; but to enjoy the complete benefit, you had to get it from his own mouth, with that delicious Irish twirl. His advertisements in cold type fail to do him justice. Don Mateo, when I first knew him, was about sixty years old, weighing close on to one-hundred and eighty—not with a big paunch on him, but just hearty. One of his physical peculiarities was that his two middle incisors, upper, were set rather far apart; that is, there was a little slit between them. This he had doubtless found of considerable advantage in his youth in the matter of accurate and long-distance expectoration. And the knack so early acquired he had improved upon with age. He was the most accomplished and artistic spitter I ever saw—nothing vulgar or nasty about it, you understand, for he was not a tobacco chewer, but I used to think he employed it as sort of lubrication and punctuation for his elegant flow of language. He usually punctuated at the end of a forceful expression; sometimes it was what

---

[14]Newmark, pp. 291-292.

Spring Street—looking south from Temple Block about 1876. The *Herald* office is in right foreground, the *Express* office in left foreground, and the Court House just off left center.

The Mirror Printing Office about 1875, in the Downey Block at Temple and New High streets. Here Spalding began his work for the Los Angeles *Times* in 1885.

the printers call "an astonisher" after an exclamation, a big word or a "Dang"—which was his favorite profanity. I am at a loss to express this fundamental element of his speech in any word or character of the English language, but suppose we just call it "st"—which comes near expressing the sound, while falling far short of suggesting the effect. I bet Don Mateo could have hit three shots out of five a fly on the wall at a distance of ten feet, and gone right on talking as though nothing unusual was happening.

As previously remarked, Don Mateo had a large vineyard and a winery fronting on Alameda Street, and he made wine on an extensive scale, and of several different kinds. His *Major Domo* was Henry Stuhr, an Austrian, with a thorough old-country education in such matters, and as Don Mateo backed him up with a plenty of money and gave him all the latitude he required, Henry turned out some very choice brands—port, claret, sherry, muscatel, hock, and a particular kind of his own devising, an amber-colored wine that was a sort of combination of muscatel and sherry, and had all the excellent qualities of both, and then some. This last named *chef d'oeuvre* Don Mateo called El Dorado.

Such a fine reputation had Don Mateo's vintage acquired that he made shipments by water, all the way round the Horn, to New York and even to London. The business had prospered and reached out so promisingly about the time of which I am writing that Don Mateo set up a business manager—Mr. Matthews, a young Englishman of active, progressive temperament and large ideas. Matthews celebrated his advent and introduced himself to the public by giving a "Harvest Home," which I suppose was a sort of old country festival to rejoice over the gathering of the crops. The affair was held in Don Mateo's great winery, and to say that it was attended by the *elite* of the town is expressing it mildly. Everybody who liked good wine and good fellowship— and all conceded that Matthews was a good fellow—was there with his wife or his sweetheart. There was a bountiful spread of goods things to eat, and Don Mateo's wine flowed like ——, but I lack the proper simile. However, there was no drunkenness or rowdyism, and after the supper we danced. It was a great affair, altogether, and after that Matthews was almost as popular as Don Mateo himself. Of course the press was well represented at the "Harvest Home," and there were some ornate reports of it in the papers, you may be sure. That was what Mr. Matthews wanted—advertising.

He had great notions as to the value of printers' ink. How he connected it up with Don Mateo's customers in New York and London, I never took the trouble to inquire. I think it was Creighton who encouraged these enterprising ideas of the English manager, and helped to confirm him in the notion that the reason why Don Mateo had not made a greater success long ago was that he was too retiring in his disposition—old-fogyish, shall we say?—and had not kept himself enough before the public. At any rate, Matthews came around pretty soon and talked matters over with us in a heart-to-heart fashion—said his own idea was publicity—lots of it; that, of course, we knew where *he* stood— but Don Mateo was—well, a little peculiar, don't you know— not quite up with modern, enterprising ways of business. Matthews suggested, with some apparent hesitation, that, while it was hard to get an appropriation of ready cash from Don Mateo for advertising, if there was anything in the way of stock that we could use, that came more particularly within his province, and he felt at liberty to make contracts. It is needless to add that we made contracts right away; not showing too much exuberance about it, of course, but mainly because we wanted to encourage a great local industry, and help bring the blooming success that the new and enterprising manager so richly deserved. We persuaded Matthews to take a double-column ad, and that was a very considerable spread, those times. "For," we said, "if you're going to hit at all, it pays to hit hard." So Matthews concluded to hit hard.

It was a whole month before anything was coming on the contract, and a long month at that, but we thought it best not to crowd the mourners. When the time for collection came round, we received a nice, trim iron-bound case (one of the kind used for long-distance shipment), and I dropped in at Prager's queensware establishment and bought a cut-glass decanter and some beautiful little iridescent goblets. As if iridescence could add anything to the sheen of Don Mateo's El Dorado!

I do not remember whether Major Ben Truman, of the *Star*, was in on the deal, but if not, he missed one of the great opportunities of his life. The *Herald* and the *Republican* (Creighton's paper) were in it to the extent of as many double-columns, next-to-reading-matter, as Mr. Matthews chose to order, and besides, we kept the public fully advised in our local columns of the goings and comings of Don Mateo Keller, of his shipments to New York and London; of the great popularity that his wines were achieving, and the growing demand. And, next to Don Mateo, Mr. Matthews, the enterprising manager, was the most notable man in town. You may be sure we filled on our end of the contract. This very pleasant arrangement went on for several months. I have no recollection of a second "Harvest Home," so the presumption is that the publicity campaign lasted less than a year. It was terminated very suddenly and unexpectedly, I know, by the receipt of peremptory orders to discontinue the double-column ad. No reason assigned—no explanation—no nothing! We did not think it worth while to look up Mr. Matthews, or to remonstrate with Don Mateo. But it was evident that the silver cord was loosed, the golden bowl was broken, the pitcher broken at the fountain, and the wheel broken at the cistern.

When I was visiting with Don Mateo, some time later, he fell into a reminiscent mood with respect to his late manager, and said:

"The danged fellah! (st) he would have turned my whole establishment into literature! (st)"

I stated some way back that Prudent Beaudry subdivided and opened for settlement the northwest, hilly portion of the city. He had been a leading merchant of the town for many years, with a store on Los Angeles Street, near Commercial, and, having accumulated a considerable fortune, retired from merchandising, and invested in those hill lands, which he got for a song, and set out to make the property valuable. It was this enterprise that Don Mateo Keller had in mind in his advertisement of 1861, when he referred to the "intrepid Beaudry," and said he proposed to "open a street to let the light of day shine in on his dark domain." Beaudry tried to get the City Council to open his streets, but it was no go; they wouldn't turn a spadeful of dirt for him. Then he graded the streets himself. He was a member of the old water company, and tried to get that organization to put in a high service, and supply his section with domestic water, but that was no go. Then he quarreled with the company, sold his stock, and built his own system of water-works. His plant was located on Alameda Street, near where North Main Street comes in, and adjoining the site where Naud's warehouse was subsequently built. An excavation in the sandy ground at that point developed a good supply of clear water, probably the underflow of the river, and over this spring he built a large roof. From the spring the water was forced by steam pumps through a long line of pipe to one of the highest hills, where there was a large, covered receiving reservoir. Thus, the water was entirely protected from the sun, no green scum formed upon it, there was no chance for contamination, and it was altogether the most wholesome supply in the city. But the works were no sooner in successful operation than the old water crowd, who looked with a jealous eye upon Beaudry's independent scheme, set up a hue and cry about the water being impure and dangerous. They based their conclusion, I think, on the fact that the water came from the ground, and was *liable* to be contaminated, forgetting that their own supply came largely from the ground and was then passed through a long open ditch into an open reservoir, where it was held indefinitely, open to the sun, and subject to all sorts of contamination. And the funny thing about it was that the objectors were able to draw from one of the good, sober-minded, conscientious doctors of the town (Dr. J. P. Widney), a long, learned opinion that the Beaudry supply might be dangerous. But the "intrepid Beaudry" was not to be beaten by such a shallow subterfuge, and the people themselves exercised their common sense. Lots in the hills gradually sold, and a few houses were built, and when the movement was not fast enough to suit him, Beaudry himself built half a dozen nice cottages on desirable lots, and sold them at auction. Don Mateo had sized him up about right; he was intrepid.[15]

The principal thoroughfares leading into the hill section from the old town were Temple and Second streets, and there was also ingress from Fifth Street, but the last named was considered away out in the suburbs. The principal thoroughfare leading across the hills, north and south, was Bunker Hill Avenue, which followed the natural contour (backbone) of the hill, and did not require grading. As the heavy cutting and filling necessary on Temple and Second streets had been done at private expense on private property, the city council refusing to have anything to do with it, the usual precautions for drainage, which the engineering department looks after, were neglected, and when the heavy rains came on, considerable ponds formed, and the water remained a long time. There was such a pond south of Temple Street, near its crossing of Fort Street, now North Broadway, opposite the northwest corner of the Court House grounds. I remember an occasion when a man drove his team into that pond, either to water the horses or wash the wagon, and both team and wagon went down and were lost.

There was another such pond north of Second Street at the

<hr/>

[15]The stories on the completion of Beaudry's water works which appeared in the *Herald*, May 28 and Aug. 15, 1874, were very likely written by Spalding.

crossing of Olive, which latter street was not graded, and, at the point named was a deep hollow. In the adobe and clay soil which formed its bed the water never did soak entirely away, and evaporation proved an endless process of elimination. The result was that the water became foul, accumulated a green scum, bred mosquitoes and bullfrogs, and was a nuisance to the neighborhood. The people living in that vicinity made a fuss and appealed to the council, but got no relief. The City Health Officer reported against it, but nothing was done. The council, having taken a stand against the improvement of the hills, seemed bent on maintaining a consistent record.

And, by the way, it was not the same council which was mentioned previously. Another had been elected. This one transacted its business in one language, but was equally inefficient. It was a pied lot of pipers, to be sure. There was B. Cohn, the chairman and the brainiest of the bunch, short and broad and deep, a regular basso-profundo, weighing about two hundred pounds—maybe two hundred and twenty-five. There was Uncle Jimmy Potts, weighing about ninety-six pounds or maybe ninety-seven, who knew everything and talked with a squeak. There was Green, the wind-mill man, a good sort of western farmer, and Tom Leahy, a lank, good natured Tipperary man, and Jake Kuhrts—but I must be careful of what I say about him, for a better friend I do not possess in this great big city. They were all friends of mine, for that matter, and they wouldn't mind a little joshing from me if they were here. They were used to it in the old days.[16]

Well, the long and short of it is that I concluded to see what I could do towards abolishing that Second Street frog pond, because I lived in that neighborhood myself. So I prepared an article headed "A Nocturnal Council," in which, after locating and describing the pond in question, and giving something of a history of the efforts to abate it, I referred to the tired reporter,

---

[16]Bernard Cohn was in the early seventies a partner in the grocery firm of Hellman, Haas & Company. Newmark (p. 595) called him "a man of much importance, both as a merchant and a City Father." He was city councilman in 1876-1878, 1880-1882, and 1887-1889; also president of the council and mayor, 1878.

Elisha K. Green, a pump and windmill agent, served on the city council 1876-1878 and 1879-1881.

Thomas Leahy, a dealer in boots and shoes, was city councilman from 1874 to 1877.

"Big, husky, hearty Jacob Kuhrts, by birth a German . . . , left home, as a mere boy, for the sea, visiting California on a vessel from China as early as 1848, and rushing off to Placer County on the outbreak of the gold-fever" (Newmark, p. 228). Returning to Los Angeles, he became a successful groceryman and served at various times in the 1870's and 1880's as city councilman, superintendent of streets, chief of the fire department, and fire commissioner.

going home from a long, extra, evening session of the city fathers, and this is what happened:

When within easy distance, there fell upon our ear a Babel of sounds—not altogether unfamiliar—which suggested that the denizens of the pond were in conclave. It might have been a greenback convention; or possibly a singing-school, or a jubilee, or an indignation meeting. The language of this amphibious tribe, partaking somewhat of the character of the Chinese in musical elements, it is not always easy to distinguish singing from talking, or talking from singing.

A little nearer, and there came from the pond a measured baritone voice, singing,

"Cohn—Cohn—Cohn—Cohn—Cohn."

The sound seemed oddly familiar, and we stopped and listened more attentively. Just then another voice—a sort of mezzo-soprano—which made about 3-4 time, and moved off with a hop, skip and a jump, chimed in:

"Potts—Potts—Potts, Potts, Potts—Potts, Potts—Potts."

The concussion with which these funny little monosyllables was ejected sounded precisely like the popping of a cork, and nothing could have been in greater contrast with the deep-mouthed "Cohn—Cohn—" which was first heard. Then, before half a second had elapsed, there came another variation, this time a shrill treble, with two distinct, ear-piercing syllables:

"Lea-hy, Lea-hy, Lea-hy, Lea-hy, Lea-hy."

What a curious kind of warble it was, to be sure! But this had hardly died away ere another followed, which was different from any of the preceding. It was a kind of hoarse rattle and croak combined, which became extremely unpleasant to the nerves.

"Kurtz-ze-Kurtz-erxe-erxe-erxe-Kurtz."

After this a very still small voice responded from a distant part of the pool:

"Work-man—Work-man—Work-man."

And another, a little more pronounced and tuneful:

"Green-n-n-n-n, Green-n-n-n-n."

Then they all seemed to join in a chorus, and it was:

"Potts, Lea-hy, Cohn—Potts, Lea-hy, Cohn—Potts, Lea-hy, Cohn," the cadence rising and falling in graceful melody, and then, quickly following, "Kurtz-e-erxe-e-erxe, Work-man, Green-n-n-n."

This grand swell seemed to conclude the chorus, and an alto solo put in glibly,

"Fill-it-up; fill-it-up-up-up-up-fill-it-fill-it-fill."

Then a full chorus came again, which, however, varied from the first in that the singers all seemed to be piping at once, making that feature in music called broken time. It is very hard to reproduce, but it ran something like this:

"Lea—Potts-hy, Cohn—Fill-Kurtz-fill-Green-oh-Green."

The voice from the other side of the pond came in mildly again:

"No-they-won't; no-they-won't; no-they-won't-un't- un't- un't. No they won't."

The frogs were no doubt giving a grand opera.[17]

When the Council held its session the next Thursday the members were all laughing and joshing each other about the frog-pond, and, by jing! one of the first things they did after coming to order was to instruct the City Engineer to build a drain under Second Street at Olive. And I, blushing like a bride, thanked them for it.

[17]Here again Spalding edited his original newspaper version, *Express*, Oct. 13, 1877.

Chapter V

INDUSTRIES AND LAND BOOMING
(1874-1878)

SPEAKING ABOUT THE encouragement of new industries, I
am reminded of George B. Davis and his Alden Fruit Drier.
Davis was an Englishman, that is, born in the old country,
but a long time here, and a naturalized citizen. He was well-to-
do, fat—rather too fat—and fussy, but a great manager. The
Alden Drying, or Dessicating, process, as they called it, had recently been sprung on the country, and factories were building
at various points to take advantage of the new order in food pres-
ervation. One was erected in Anaheim about the same time. Davis
had secured the concession for Los Angeles, had purchased the
necessary machinery, and proceeded to construct an ample building on the right—no, I mean the left bank of the Los Angeles
River, near the Macy Street bridge. I always get confused about
that right and left when it comes to a river, and have to think
twice whether I am facing with the stream or against the stream
when I say it. And the Los Angeles River at that point, especially
in summer, was bothersome when one wanted to determine the
direction of the current. It is better now [ca. 1930], since the
Owens River water has been turned in. But I am getting away
off the flow of my subject.

The Drier building was big and barny, skimped as to windows, tall, and looked much like a grain elevator that had stopped a little shy of full development. Davis had money, all right, or he could not have done all those things, but whether it was his own money or that of a company, I never learned. At any rate, he was the only man in sight, in connection with the enterprise, and he was very much in sight. Like the active Mr. Matthews before mentioned, he believed in publicity, and early called at the office to let us know that he had gone into the enterprise, and what he proposed to do. He let us have printed matter, descriptive of the Alden process, and what it was capable of doing, and how it was going to revolutionize things, and of course with such easy copy, on a perfectly legitimate, new local industry, we gave him columns and columns. As the work of building progressed, he dropped in occasionally—say two or three times a week—to report progress, and replenish our stack of reprint, and in a little time the name of George B. Davis became as much of a household word as had been that of Don Mateo Keller.

Well, the factory was completed at last, and the machinery installed, and representatives of the press were given a preliminary peek at the establishment, and there were more columns of jubilation over "Our Fine New Alden Drier." Although I fail to find any of this interesting literature pasted in my old scrap book, I can give from memory a pretty fair outline of the process and the mechanism. The latter consisted of several big flues, or chimneys, ranged along one side of the building, extending from the basement to the roof, and inside each flue there was an elevating system, operated by power, which carried large trays of prepared fruit or vegetables or meat, or what not, upward, upward, upward—slowly while it was giving its moisture to the moderately heated air inside. When a particular tray that had been inserted in the basement or on the ground floor reached the top story, the delicatessen thereon were as dry and hard as so many walnuts—and more wrinkled. At the time I could have given the percentage of moisture that had been eliminated from each kind of comestible so beautifully preserved. I am sorry I have lost that data, and must beg the pardon of the reader for not presenting it here. An outsider might not have known, but we gentlemen of the press knew, from our extensive editing and proof-reading on the subject, that the dried and wrinkled and warped objects that were taken from the tray on the top floor needed only to have that certain percentage of moisture restored—in other words, to be soaked—and they would become, to all intents and purposes, as good as new. One of the strongest points in the Alden process was that it dried almost anything under the sun, and a good deal better and quicker than the sun could do it. I am not sure, however, whether it could have dessicated some of the sermons we used to get in those days since they were so much so already; I would have hesitated to try one of "Aunt Polly's" discourses as a first effort.

As soon as everything was running smoothly, and a good variety of substantials and delicacies accumulated, the rotund and glowing George B. Davis announced a banquet—an invitation affair, of course, and very select—to demonstrate the excellencies of his evaporated products, and show the factory in operation. Of course the members of the press were in it, and back of it, and all through it; they felt like sponsors for the enterprise, and almost part owners. George B. Davis even consulted us about the invitations. He wanted substantial citizens, men of account in the community, you know, and their wives; oh, yes, surely! for women are interested in such matters a good deal more than men. I myself had *carte blanche*, to invite as many people as I chose, and you may be certain all of my particular friends were remembered—Fred, and Andy, and George and Mac and several others. If they were not substantial citizens, I would like to know who were. I felt quite a glow of pride about inviting my friends, as a member of the press and one who in a humble way, so to speak, had contributed what I could towards this grand climax.

The banquet came off according to schedule, and there was a large crowd. George B. Davis had secured the services of a *chef* and an adequate force of assistants and servitors. After sufficient time to inspect the works, and see their operation, and examine the evaporated delicatessen, and ask all sorts of questions, and receive all sorts of answers from George B. Davis and those of us who were best informed on the subject, the company were seated at a long table in the ample space on the main floor. The banquet was unique, as was intended, and as everybody expected it to be. If my recollection is accurate, there was no soup, because, of course, nobody could expect that to come from a Drier, but there were a plenty of other things that were equivalent, and entirely compensated for its absence. The plan of George B. Davis was that every one of the viands—except the wine and the bread and butter—should represent one of the products of the process; should, indeed, *be* a product of his own factory. His ambition was to show the great scope of the Alden method. There were fish and meat—beef, mutton, pork, duck, chicken, turkey; everything, you know—and vegetables—potatoes, carrots, turnips, cauliflower, cabbage, celery, pumpkin, squash, and all that end-less line; and beyond came the fruits (in or out of season didn't make any difference to the Alden process). However, no attempt was made on lettuce. And furthermore, it was the ambition of George B. Davis that each guest should be served with a little sample of each viand—not a great lot, you know; he didn't want to surfeit them; just a little spoonful, and then, if they desired more, they could come back. So, at first we got a moderate help-ing of fish—there may have been three or four or five kinds, but if so, it was immaterial—it all looked alike and you couldn't have told oysters from salmon, because it was cooked into a sort of gruel, and they all ran together anyhow. We were glad when the plates were changed, for it gave us a new start, and we deter-mined, next time, to keep better track of things. When the meats came on, one after the other, through the whole imperative *menu*, it was worse, and more of it—and the vegetables on top of that! You might dabble your fork in a little puddle on one side of your plate, thinking you were getting chicken, and maybe it would turn out squash, as nearly as you could tell—or maybe turnip—which was it? If a dish of gravy were set before you for a meal, and you tried to eat it with your knife and fork, or even your spoon, you wouldn't be able to get very far; now, would you? And if you had forty-six kinds of gravy put down in little spoonfuls on your plate, do you think you could keep track of each different kind, when the geographical boundaries had co-alesced and been practically obliterated?

It seemed to me that George B. Davis's *chef* had got his per-centages mixed; had really restored more humidity to the several items of delicatessen than belonged to them—more in fact than the Drier had taken out. At any rate the fish and meat and vege-tables that were served to us—if they were fish and meat and so forth—resembled original chaos in that they were without form, and void.

As for George B. Davis and his Alden Drier, we never men-tioned either one of them again in our columns. The scheme was a flat failure, of course, and in a little time George B. Davis faded out. He went without comment from the press. Maybe that is why I did not paste up anything about him in my scrap book.[1]

[1]The story of George B. Davis and the Alden Drier actually covered a long period of time. On April 3, 9, and 16, 1874, the *Herald* raised the question of introducing the Alden fruit drying process into Los Angeles. On August 4 the paper announced the arrival of George B. Davis and his plans for the Alden concession. Through August, September, and October at least fifteen articles elaborated on the progress, including

About that time my conscience began to get troublesome on the matter of drinking. I saw that a newspaper man was subject to great temptation, and could not help noting how many of them, even the brightest and apparently the strongest, fell by the wayside. Concluding that there was no safe ground short of absolute teetotalism, and that this might best be accomplished by putting a formal restraint upon myself, I made application for membership in Merrill Lodge, Good Templars.[2] The name went through the process of election, and I was duly initiated. But I never attended a meeting of the lodge afterward, mainly because the exigencies of business prevented. The lodge held its meetings in the evening, one night a week, and the evening was always my busiest time. I remained a member of the lodge for perhaps a year, during which I faithfully kept the pledge, and did not find it a serious handicap in my business or an irksome restraint. But I was paying dues for something from which no social advantage was derived, and mature reflection convinced me that a man must rely on his own moral force for protection from the temptations of life, so I sent in my resignation from the lodge, which was accepted; they called it a demit.

A few months afterward the Pomona tract was opened for sale and settlement.[3] As was usual with those booming schemes, the company first built a nice little hotel in the center of the tract, where they expected the town to be, and then gave a blow-out, to which the public was invited, to formally launch the enterprise. I attended, as representative of the *Herald*, to write up the affair, and at the dinner served in the hotel, drank a glass of beer. Now it happened that Jesse Yarnell was also present, representing the little *Mirror*, or the job office, or perhaps both. We did not consider him exactly a representative of the press, but treated him as a hail fellow whenever he went along. Jesse was nothing if not a partizan for the temperance cause, and he saw

---

some grandiose paeans ending "God bless Alden!" The report on the commencement of operations came Oct. 22, 1874. But the dinner for the press and guests did not occur until a year and a half later: *Herald*, May 23, 1876.

Two sections of Spalding's account have been omitted from the text: one, the story of a spilled plate at the banquet and, two, a long disquisition on the nature and value of food drying.

[2]The Order of Good Templars, an international society of abstainers, was founded in 1851 in Utica, New York, but by the 1880's was active in Europe, Asia, and South America, as well as the United States. The Los Angeles branch was founded in 1868 and in 1875 claimed 220 members, according to the city directory of that year.

[3]According to Spalding's Diary this was about November 1875. The story on the Pomona excursion, or a most similar one, appears in the *Herald*, Feb. 22, 1876.

me drink that glass of beer. Without saying a word to me on the subject, or conveying an admonition in any way, he reported the matter to headquarters. The result was that I soon received a formal notice to appear before the lodge and explain my conduct. Probably if I had gone in and expressed contrition, and promised to do better in future, they would have forgiven me with a mild reprimand. But I considered that, after withdrawing from the lodge, I was out of its jurisdiction. So I merely wrote a letter declining to appear, and in real polite language, which was intended to be caustic, independent, and even defiant, virtually told the lodge to go to thunder. The result was that my withdrawal was revoked—I was voted back into the lodge, and then expelled. But I didn't care much for that crowd of cranks, anyway, so bore up as bravely as possible under the disgrace. I am sorry, however, that I did not keep a copy of that letter. It would probably look funny now, and the readers of this veracious history might enjoy a smile at my expense.[4]

[Hall of
Merrill Lodge No. 299
I.O.G.T.

Los Angeles, Dec. 4 '75
Bro. Spaulding
    Dear Sir:
        You are hereby ordered to appear at the next regular meeting of this lodge to be held next Sat. evening for trial on a charge of violation of Art II of our Constitution.

Yours in F. H. & C.
Calvin L. Porter
Seal.   W. Sec.

Calvin L. Porter,
    W. Sec.
        Merrill Lodge No. 299 I.O.G.T.
Dear Sir:
        I am in receipt of your note of 4th inst. ordering me to appear at the next regular meeting of your Lodge for trial on the charge of violation of Art II of your Constitution.
        I shall decline to conform to your command on the following grounds:
    1st I am not a member of your Lodge, and
    2d   As a consequence your Lodge has no authority or right to try me for the violation of anything.

[4]Spalding had copied the following letters into his Diary, and they are reproduced from that source.

[73]

Some months ago, I received a card of honorable dismissal from Merrill Lodge No. 299 which, as I understood it, severed my connection with that organization. What the purport of your Article I, II or III may be, I am unable to say as I am not familiar with your Constitution or the workings of your Order. I believe, while a member, I had not the honor of attending a meeting throughout and was never in the lodge room but two or three times. But, whatever the obligations of your Constitution are, I am well aware that, in common usage, they are considered absolved by those who have severed their connection with the Lodge; and, in proof of this, I can cite several respectable citizens of this place.

When I was waited upon by a committee of your Lodge a few weeks ago and informed that charges had been preferred against me, I freely surrendered my card of dismissal, being unwilling to cast reproach upon the Lodge in any way. This surrender, I was informed by your committee, would answer your demands upon me in full. Now, it seems, the affair must be raked forth anew and your honorable body exercised in an attempt to expel a person who does not belong to it. This, I regard as a gratuitous insult—an effort on the part of a few members of Merrill Lodge to drag my name into dishonorable notoriety simply for the purpose of gratifying a petty malice. This, of course, I must allow you to do if it suits your pleasure but I must beg you to excuse me from appearing before your august tribunal, and I can only hope that your satisfaction in the disposal of this case may be as great as my indifference to the good or bad opinion of your Lodge.

I remain, sir,

Very respectfully

Wm. A. Spalding]

At the time Pomona was thus auspiciously opened to the public, it had but one building—the hotel previously mentioned—and the rest was just bare, open plain. Nobody could then foresee the great possibilities in it, or the fine city that would result some years later. But the community saw through a glass darkly, and worked by faith to a great extent in those old days. The founding of Pomona dates in 1887.[5]

Colton was opened to the public in the same year [1875], and came about in this way: The Southern Pacific Railway company, in extending its line to the east, demanded from the city of San Bernardino a considerable subsidy as a condition for running through that place. San Bernardino couldn't see it in that light, and so the Southern Pacific laid its track four miles to the southward. Colton was projected as a rival to San Bernardino, but it never proved very formidable. Which side was heavier loser by the transaction, it is hard to tell, but probably the railroad was

---

[5]I.e., the incorporation of the city, Dec. 31, 1887.

the more short-sighted. When the rival Santa Fe came along, it not only ran through San Bernardino gratis, but made quite an important point of the place, locating its main California shops there, and getting the lion's share of its business. When I attended the opening for Colton, it was just a barren sandy plain, with only two buildings. One of them was occupied by a newspaper, the weekly *Semi-Tropic*, which must have been subsidized by the railroad company, for there was no other patronage in sight; the other was a saloon. How those two institutions could exist side-by-side in that bleak, sandy place, and not eat each other up, I could not make out.[6]

San Fernando was laid off by Senator Charles Maclay, owner of the old ranch of San Fernando, comprehending a large acreage.[7] It was in 1874, when the Southern Pacific had just built its line to that point, and was getting ready to begin its long tunnel through the mountains to the northward. I attended Senator Maclay's picnic opening when there was no building in sight but the railroad station and the wreck of the old mission. The surrounding lands seemed as sandy and bleak as at Colton. There was an auction sale, and a few sanguine people bought lots. I suspicioned that they were by-bidders. I wrote up as favorable an account of the affair as I could, putting the principal stress on the social features of the picnic.[8] The next time Senator Maclay met

[6]"The excursion to Colton was for the purpose of selling lots in the newly laid-out town, and I went along to write it up. Of course I put it up in as favorable a light as possible—that's business—and, between me and the red book, I do think it as choice a piece of desert as I ever set eyes on." Spalding's Diary, [Nov. 1875]. The Colton newspaper was probably the *Advocate*, since the *Semi-Tropic* did not begin until 1877.

[7]Charles Maclay, native of Massachusetts, came to California in the early fifties. For a while he was a tanner in Santa Cruz, then came south, entered politics, and became a state senator. Newmark, p. 459.

[8]"A Flying Trip to San Fernando" (excerpts of which are quoted in Ch. IV), printed in the *Herald*, May 6, 1874, commented on the development of the new town. In his *History*, I, 208, Spalding described Maclay's promotional efforts in greater detail: "In the spring Senator Charles Maclay, in connection with George K. and F. B. Porter, purchased the San Fernando rancho of 56,000 acres, including the old Mission property. The Southern Pacific Railroad was building its line northward from Los Angeles, and when it reached a point near the old Mission Senator Maclay selected that for a town site, calling it San Fernando. As soon as the railroad station was built the Senator had a big whoop-up, inviting everybody to go up and see his new town and participate in a free barbecue. There was a considerable crowd, and a band of music enlivened the occasion. A plat of the town was in evidence, and some attempt was made at an auction sale of lots, but the crowd was not very enthusiastic."

Newmark (p. 459) took a more optimistic view of San Fernando: "Within a couple of weeks, hundreds of lots were sold and the well-known colony was soon on the way to prosperity."

Similar stories that may have been Spalding's appeared on April 21 and July 16 and 17, 1874.

me, he handed me two deeds, one conveying a lot to me, and one to George Safford, book-keeper of the *Herald*, who had accompanied the expedition. After consulting George, I handed the deeds back to the senator, and told him our paper didn't allow us to take tips. The real reason was that we would not take those lots, even as a gift. But the deeds must have been recorded by the generous and persistent donor, for we used to find our names in the delinquent tax list for several years afterward. Thus do they of little faith turn their backs on good fortune, when it knocks on the door, and is even insistent on entering.

When the Southern Pacific line to the eastward had got as far as the town of Spadra there was a grand barbecue and jubilation given by Uncle Billy Rubottom, the popular Boniface of that burg.[9] It was largely attended, and proved a memorable affair. There was no attempt to boom the place other than to give an old-fashioned southern feast and jollification. If anybody had offered me a lot, gratis, at Spadra, I would have accepted, with due thanks. Yet Spadra never had a boom, and a lot there is worth not much more now than it was then. As Josh Billings observed, "You can never tell how far a frog is going to jump till you tickle it with a straw."

The Azusa Rancho was purchased by one of the early boom companies, the land subdivided into farms, and a town was planned to be located on the site of the old Dalton homestead, to be known as Mound City. That was years and years before the first real boom in Southern California—in fact, it was premature —we were ready for it, but the rest of the world was not. I went out with a party of the projectors to look the property over and write it up.

The Daltons were still living in the old homestead, which was located on top of a little hill, solitary, in the midst of the gently sloping mesa all round—the same little hill upon which the Union High School now stands, only it was higher then, and not graded or terraced. There was a capacious *zanja* that ran around the hill near its base, and furnished facilities for irrigating a vine-yard of thirty or forty acres on the comparatively level ground to the northwest. A few trees of various sorts were growing along the line of the ditch, and on the northeast there was an old olive

---

[9]William Rubottom founded Spadra, which he named after his home town in Arkansas. Newmark (pp. 144-145) described Uncle Billy as famous for fifteen years presiding over his barbecues in shirt sleeves. Spalding's account of the Spadra opening was in the *Herald*, June 2, 1874.

James J. Ayers

Harrison Gray Otis

orchard of two or three acres. As water could not be made to run up hill, there were no trees around the house, and the whole hill, in fact, was pretty bare except for the buildings, and they were bare also. There probably was domestic water, pumped by a windmill from the *zanja*, and elevated to a tank behind the house, but it did not seem to occur to the old-timers that such water could be used for irrigation—there was not enough of it—and such a thing as a lawn or flower garden was not expected on the big ranches. There were corrals for horses, cattle and sheep, but they could hardly be accounted ornamental. The residence was a long, one-story adobe of conventional design, and in interior arrangement consisted of one ample room adjoining the next from one end to the other—no halls or corridors, but each room opening into its neighbor by a door. The lack of interior means of communication without violating the privacy of bedrooms was obviated by having outside doors in most of the rooms, leading to the front or rear court. These courts, for a little space, were paved with small cobble stones, no doubt gathered from the wash not far distant; and beyond the courts for another limited space there were walks, laid out in fanciful curves, and neatly inclosed, each side, with rows of the same cobbles. In the more or less fanciful beds lying between the walks there may have been a few shrubs and plants, but only such, one could see, as the women of the family might keep alive through the summer by using a watering pot. There was no evidence of water under pressure, or a hose, or any such nonsensical city contraption. A considerable distance from the house, on the northeast, there was a large stable with adobe walls, and another ample building of the same sort for a wagon house and shop. On the north, there was a big build-ing which we were told was the winery, though we were not invited to inspect the inside of it. There were various other build-ings of minor proportions, evidently for the storage of grain and the odds and ends of a large ranch.

We passed the remnant of the day, after eating the lunch which had been brought along, in driving and walking about the ranch, though there was not much of interest to see after leaving the Dalton grounds and vineyard until we arrived in the squatter settlement, a mile or two to the southeast. There we found little farms, with cheap wooden houses, the land mostly under culti-vation, and growing crops of corn, pumpkins, etc. It was there I was struck with the wonderful fertility of the soil, for we saw corn standing ten or twelve feet high, and other crops propor-tionally luxuriant. That impression abided with me a long time, and was destined to have an important bearing on my life, though I did not dream of it at the time. The squatters, we were told, were all Americans, land-hungry, who had come in and taken advantage of an apparent flaw in title, pre-empted, settled and improved individual pieces, and were holding their own, in spite of perennial law-suits brought by old man Dalton to eject them. It was the expense of these years of litigation, and the inability to keep up interest on the large sums he borrowed, which had finally wrecked his fortunes, and compelled him to sell everything. At one time he had owned, or at least held, all the land from the head of the valley, from the Sierra Madre mountains on the north to the Puente hills on the south, as far down, and including the Santa Anita Ranch, now owned by the Baldwin heirs. Piece by piece he had parted with it to satisfy his creditors and the courts and lawyers, and now that he had given up the Azusa Ranch, he did not possess a square rod of land, or a dollar. He was given a few acres by the purchasing company a mile or so down the line of his own old ditch, a little wooden shack was built for him, and there he passed his last days. But I am getting away ahead of my story.[10]

There was no room in the Dalton house to accommodate us, even if we had asked, so, after eating supper from our hamper and smoking the traditional camper's pipe, we prepared to make down our beds in the ample haystack that stood near the barn. Bedding had been brought along for the purpose. I had never slept out of doors before, and like most novices was impressed with the danger of freezing to death. So I kept my clothing on, found a good spot on top of the haystack, wrapped myself well in the blankets, and went to it. There was no trouble about going to sleep in those days, and especially after such an unusual jaunt in the country. I trust that the reader will pardon the rhapsody which is usually expected from such an experience with respect to the beautiful dome of heaven, the winking stars and the crescent or gibbous moon, just —— and you know the rest. They may have been there—no doubt they were visible to the naked eye— but I did not see them. It was my own fault, and I have been sorry for it ever since. If one loses the opportunity for his first impression, you know, it is gone forever. But I do know that, along about midnight, I awakened, gasping for breath, and

[10]Henry Dalton, an Englishman, had been a merchant in Peru before coming to southern California in the 1840's. By the 1870's he owned thousands of acres in addition to the Azusa Ranch. In 1881 he lost the Azusa by foreclosure on the mortgage and moved to the small house which Spalding described. Dalton died in 1884.

steaming from every pore. The heaviest portion of my body had gone down in that yielding hay, and I was doubled up like a hinge. I jumped or rolled from the top of that stack, unwinding myself as I went, and after reaching solid earth, it took quite a little time to restore normal respiration and reduce temperatures. I purposely use the plural, because I was hot in various places. While this process of resuscitation was going on I had time to indulge in a practical thought or two, and then I took from the stack an armful of hay, put it right down on the hard ground where I stood, shed a part of my clothing, wrapped myself up to a reasonable degree, and lay down again. Just like that! And there was nothing more to it until the boys began to stir about at daylight, and I waked up. One of the crowd asked how I came to be down off the haystack—there will always be such observant and troublesome fellows along with almost any party, you know—and I told him he was mistaken; I had gone to sleep on the ground. Which was true of the second time. And I brazened it out that way.

While the volunteer cook was getting breakfast, a couple of us took the shot guns and sauntered out a little way to see what we could find. My associate hunter went in the direction of the corral, and I down along the ditch. We had not been separated more than five minutes when I heard a bang in his direction, and on the instant came a flock of wild doves that settled on one bank of the ditch in as straight a line as a rank of soldiers could dress-parade. I was only a little distance off at one end of the line, which gave me an enfilading fire, and I banged away. There were seven dead doves. These I bore back to camp in triumph—it was too good to keep. But my friend was there ahead of me. It seems that he had found a flock of quail in the corral, all bunched up, feeding, and his single shot had killed twelve. Probably there had not been much hunting on the ranch for a long time. When our combined slaughter was piled together, I began to feel ashamed of both of us, and have been ashamed of that feat of mine ever since. Maybe that is the reason why I have never been much of a hunter. But I do like to catch fish.

I must have been mightily impressed with the Azusa Ranch, taking abundant notes, for the scrap-book shows that I wrote six columns about it, which were published in four installments, a column and a half a day for four days [*Express*, August 5-8, 1878], and a covert threat of more at some convenient season. Even then I failed to get in most of the graphic features contained in this simple narrative. We got a hundred dollars for that write-up, and were bound that the company should have the worth of their money.

As for the Mound City enterprise, with all of our boosting, it was a failure. Although the company offered those rich lands at thirty to fifty dollars an acre, there were no takers. After struggling along for a year or so, the company were obliged to transfer those four or five thousand acres to the Los Angeles County Bank, in satisfaction of indebtedness, losing all they had put into it of their own money. And even the bank was not happy over the acquisition. Some of the stockholders found fault with John S. Slauson, the president, for such a reckless loan, and he made a bluff at the directors to take the property off their hands for the amount of the indebtedness and accrued interest. They gladly took him up. And that is how Mr. Slauson came into possession of that land. It cost him, I presume, all of ten or twelve dollars an acre. After holding it some years, and when the times were just ripe for it, he laid off the town of Azusa, subdivided the lands about in small tracts, fixed his prices, and announced that no sales would be made until a certain day at nine o'clock a.m. [April 1, 1887] when the maps would be on view at his office, and selections could be made, "first come, first served," as Don Mateo had put it with reference to his Aliso tract long before. And, do you know that people stood in line all night in order that they might get a preference when the office opened? And John S. Slauson was not offering the land at thirty to fifty dollars an acre either. Lots in the town of Azusa went like hot cakes, along with the rest. Yet everybody knew that the town-site was on a sand, gravel and boulder wash. When somebody asked him why he had chosen such a place for the location of his center, Mr. Slauson said, "If it's not good for a town, it isn't good for anything!" After all, there is a great deal in picking your time and knowing how to handle people.

Chapter VI

A MATTER O' MARRYING
(1874-1876)

WHEN FRED AND I had our heart-to-heart talk on Bay Farm Island I told him of my tacit understanding with Mary Dennison, and he was delighted beyond measure. We three had been schoolmates together, and Fred had known for several years that my leaning had been towards Mary, but now that the inclination had become a settled purpose, and that my affection was reciprocated, it seemed to please him as much as though he had found a new sister. Although there had been only one kiss to bind the bargain between Mary and me, and nothing had been said about marrying or giving in marriage, I felt that the compact was made, signed, sealed and delivered, and never had a misgiving about its eventual consummation, provided we both lived and circumstances developed so as to make marriage possible. Fred took the matter in the same way, and never alluded to it in our confidential talks except as a foregone conclusion.

Of course I wrote to Mary immediately on my arrival in California, giving a brief account of the journey in a rather matter-of-fact way, and in closing, ventured to send my love. So staid! So formal! So aggravatingly conventional! Looking back from this distance, and considering the depth of my affection, and my sincerity of purpose, I wonder why I was so non-committal, so formal, so cold. But there is no chance of explaining the ways of a young man in love, especially the ways of one who was so uncertain as to his own future. It required a week or ten days to exchange letters, and in due time I received a missive from my sweetheart couched in just as formal terms, and with the same amount of love tacked on at the bottom. From that time forth our letters were exchanged at about the same rate, each waiting for the receipt of the other's letter before writing again. But when I obtained employment in Los Angeles, and found that I could fill the bill and make a permanency of it, I felt a little more latitude in declaring myself, albeit my letters were still rather matter-of-fact and formal.

When the burden was upon me of filling two or three columns of the paper with local news every day, and I was exercising my wits in a very dull town to find subjects for discussion, I naturally dropped back into my earlier fad of writing verses. These were generally in a lighter vein, and turned on minor incidents and comical situations and droll subjects; sometimes ridicule of an unesteemed contemporary. My verses helped to fill space, and give variety to the columns, and possibly to furnish some entertainment for readers. At any rate my editor never called me down on them; so I wrote as fancy suggested, but always anonymously or under a pseudonym.[1] It may be that some of my lighter jingles carried more sentiment than appeared on the surface, and I half suspect that what I failed to put into the letters I might have incorporated here in an obscure way, not fully realizing it myself. I was like the troubadours of ancient Provence, who wrote verses to their inamoratas without mentioning the name of the beloved object or giving any clue except one that she herself could read. Such may have been the case with the following, which was published anonymously in the *Herald*. It attempted to give a suggestion of happy, simple domestic life, such as I hoped was in store for the girl to whom I was devoted. At any rate I sent her a clipping, and she was gracious enough to say in her next letter that she liked it.[2]

[1]For his poetry he usually used the name "Pokey"; for his lighter, human-interest stories or fiction, "Adolphus Perkins." One bit of fiction which Spalding wrote under his own name was in the *Express*, Dec. 24, 1877: "Banker Watkins, a Christmas Story with a Goblin in It."

[2]The poem appeared in the *Herald*, June 28, 1874. Spalding in the "Autobiography," however, used the version that he printed in *Snatches of Song* ([Los Angeles], 1921). Only two of the twelve stanzas are included here.

Little Swallow, Flitting

Little Swallow, flitting
   To and fro,
Innocent, unwitting
   Aught of woe,
Could I be as light of heart and free,
Would I were a swallow too, with thee,
   Flitting,
     Flitting,
      Flitting to and fro,
Innocent, unwitting aught of woe.

Mud-daubed nest dependent
   From the wall,
Where the sun resplendent
   Makes his call;
Man might imitate thy simple art,
Letting sunshine into home and heart;
   Humble,
     Happy,
      Pattern for us all—
Mud-daubed nest dependent from the wall.

But a more direct appeal came in the following:

My Sunset Land

Beyond the desert's fiery breath,
   Beyond its dreary waste of sand,
Beyond its toil and pain and death,
   There is my glorious Sunset Land.

There do the living waters flow,
   There sing the birds in sweet attune;
There do the flowers in winter blow,
   There it seems always afternoon.

Abide with me in that sunset land;
   Come, dearest one, and abide with me,
And Heaven shall then be close at hand,
   And time shall but merge in eternity.

So the above will have to pass in this veracious and candid history for the more ardent phases of my love-making.

As soon as Fred and I were both on an assured salary basis, the business firm of Spalding & Wood was dissolved by mutual consent. This did not mean that our friendship was in any way affected. We still roomed together, and were Damon and Pythias. I should add, however, that by this time our intimate group had been increased to four, including the two originals and Andy Lawrence and George Safford. Andy's chum name was "Nibs," and George's "Cully." As soon as I regained my equilibrium, I began saving money for a definite end, and the astute reader can readily guess what it was. After working and saving about eighteen months, I thought my accumulation was sufficient to make the venture. Meantime by correspondence, I had brought Mary to a definite "Yes," and I had written to Father Dennison and obtained his consent and implied blessing. My little hoarding was deposited in the Temple & Workman Bank. But, in the fall of 1875 that bank closed its doors. Here was a sad to do for me. In the course of a couple of weeks, however, the management raised some money by mortgaging valuable property to E. J. Baldwin, and attempted a partial resumption.[3] That is to say, Mr. [Henry S.] Ledyard, the Cashier, opened a provisional office with the firm of H. Newmark & Co., on Los Angeles Street, and made partial payments on checks in especially meritorious and urgent cases. I called upon Mr. Ledyard, and laid all of my cards on the table. The story of a young fellow who had worked so hard to get money to be married on must have appealed to him, for he allowed me to check out all of my deposit. I may have been the only one thus summarily favored. In the final wind up of the institution, the depositors realized nothing.

[*Spalding here described the development of unfortunate financial straits for the Dennisons in Kansas City and St. Louis; as a result he concluded, "our marriage should be brought to a focus." In September 1875 he visited his family in Kansas City and then proceeded to St. Louis.*]

The Dennisons were living in rented quarters, one of those two-story brick buildings, with a whole block built just alike and close together to save ground space. Mary gave me a cordial welcome, of course, and the whole family co-operated to make the

[3]Actually the resumption began before the Baldwin loan, which was made some months later.

stranger-lover feel as much at home as possible. A few days after my arrival the family moved to another location, and Mary and I were sent to Shaw's Garden to amuse ourselves, and get our dinners where we would. It was not difficult for us to put in the time. But one amusing circumstance developed. After we had dined at a restaurant in the garden, or near it, I offered to pay the check, tendering a ten-dollar gold piece, as I had no small change. The girl looked at my coin in astonishment, and declined to receive it; she did not recognize it as money. This is explained by the fact that gold had not been in circulation in the East since the beginning of the Civil War; but we of the Pacific Coast had kept on a coin basis. So Mary came to the rescue, and paid the bill. Whether she ever got it back I do not remember. We two practical lovers returned to the old quarters in time to see the last load dispatched, and as there was a looking glass and a clock which could not be safely intrusted to the van, Mary carried one and I the other, and we walked over to the new place, a few blocks distant.

Aunt Ann, on a hasty summons, came down from Columbus, Ohio, to engineer the wedding. She brought along as a present a fine leather trunk, with "Mrs. W. A. Spalding" lettered on one end. Mrs. Elizabeth Bay, a matronly dressmaker, was brought into service, and the construction of a traveling dress and whatever accessories were required occupied the attention of the feminine household. Nothing was wasted on mere frills. In a week or ten days we were ready for the event. Dr. A. H. Burlingame, pastor of the Second Baptist Church, was called in and Mary and I stood at one end of the little parlor and went through the simple ceremony.[4] There were present as observers only Father and Mother Dennison, Brother Tom, Aunt Ann and the dressmaker. The bride and groom took a train for Kansas City immediately after the ceremony. And that is the reason the bride was married in her traveling dress. There never was a wedding with less ostentation. We staid with Father and Mother at their little home on O K Creek one day and night, and all the rest of the family rallied around to give us welcome. Then we were off for our journey to the Pacific Coast.

On the transcontinental trip we passed for a sedate couple, well seasoned to matrimony. Mary and I had made it up that there should be no public spooning or anything else to give us away, and in her sober costume she certainly did not look the conven-

[4]Oct. 14, 1875.

tional bride. The situation was made the more enjoyable because one of our fellow passengers, Mrs. Briggs, a regular Brigadier General, with a raucous voice, was openly on a hunt for a bride and groom. She had never undertaken so long a journey before without finding a new married couple, and she had an inkling that there must be such an interesting pair on the train somewhere. But a journey clear through had failed to disclose the objects of quest. She was simply disgusted. Mary and I chuckled, but said nothing, and persevered in our staid behavior.

There was a young fellow passenger named Frazier, whom I fell in with in the smoker, and with whom I became chummy. He confided in me that his home was in San Francisco; that he had been manager and factotum for the wealthy James Lick; that since the death of that worthy, he had been manager of the Lick estate; and that he had just been married, although his wife was not with him on that trip. Under this stimulus I told Mr. Frazier that I had just been married myself, and was taking my bride to a home in Los Angeles. That led to a fellow-feeling between us, and we became very good train-friends. Frazier must have let out the secret towards the last of the trip, for Brigadier General Briggs learned on the last day that she had been humbugged. "Good Lord!" she said. "A bride and groom all the while, right under our noses, and we didn't know it!" But it was then too late to make much fuss over us. Frazier asked what place we expected to stop at in San Francisco, and in compliment to him I said, "Why, I think at the Lick." So we took the Lick House bus after landing from the ferry, and in the scramble, we lost track of our Mr. Frazier. When I registered at the hotel, signing for the first time, "W. A. Spalding & Wife," the clerk sent a bell-hop to show the way, and on entering we were fairly dumbfounded by the elegance. We had been assigned to the "Bridal Chamber," the swell apartments of the hotel. I was at first of a mind to go back and tell the clerk that I could not afford such style, but on second thought [decided] that, as we were to be there only a day and night, I would be a sport and carry it off. When I came to settle my bill, however, to my astonishment, I was charged only the average rate. It was all the doing of that man Frazier. When that dawned upon me it was too late to look him up, and personally thank him for his unexpected and overwhelming courtesy. So I had to be content to leave with the clerk my compliments and thanks.

We came down by steamer, and Mary had a sorry time with sea-sickness. She was still so demoralized when we got off the boat at San Pedro that she left one shoe as a souvenir for the stewardess.

We installed ourselves at the Kimball Mansion on New High Street, where I had previously boarded. Fred and Andy were guests, and perhaps George Safford. So we were in the circle of friends at the start, and there were enough middle-aged women among the boarders to take a lively interest in the new couple—rather too much interest to suit us. So we staid only two or three weeks at the Kimball Mansion.

My friend W. W. Creighton, who had taken my place on the *Herald* during my absence, was a seasoned newspaper man from Leavenworth, Kansas. After a number of years on the press, he had served a term as City Clerk.[5] He was a widower, with a little girl, named Pearl, about five years old. He was keeping house in a cottage on Fort Street, just below Third, and employed a German girl, Emma Drexel, for housekeeper. Creighton said he had more room in the cottage than he needed, and if we would like to begin housekeeping, he could let us in. That suited us better than boarding, and we accepted the offer. We had two little front rooms and the use of the kitchen. We were in a cottage belonging to "Aunt Winnie," an old, well-to-do colored woman—no style about it, but very comfortable, and the Creighton family proved agreeable house-mates.

We lived with the Creightons several months. Some time in the summer of 1876 Mr. Beaudry held an auction sale of hill lots, and also disposed of three of his cottages on the corner of Second and Charity streets on the Crown Hill summit. I bid off the cottage on the northwest corner for the sum of $2,905. The terms were easy, and I was required to make only a small payment down. The remainder was on long time, with moderate monthly or quarterly installments. We found a family named Mayo tenants in the house, and as we did not need all of the space, made arrangements for them to remain, giving us the two small front rooms and the joint use of their kitchen. Mr. Mayo was a conductor in the employ of the Southern Pacific railway, a rotund good-natured man, and his wife of equal rotundity and bonhomie. They had no children, but living with them were a young widowed sister-in-law of Mrs. Mayo—a Mrs. Johnson—and her two sons, about eight and ten years of age. We got along nicely

[5]The mention of Creighton as city clerk apparently does not refer to Los Angeles since he does not appear in the "Chronological Record of Los Angeles City Officials, 1850-1938," typescript, 2 vols., Los Angeles Public Library.

with our tenants, and the revenue derived from them helped in meeting my installments. Thus, we were finally launched in our own home, although it had a pretty stout string attached to it. By this time I had been able to pay off my $500 debt in Kansas City, and as I was making a salary of $100 a month, we got along swimmingly.[6]

<hr />

[6]A short passage regarding Kansas City and the family has been omitted here.

Chapter VII

ANOTHER REVOLUTION: FROM *HERALD* TO *EXPRESS* (1876-1879)

JOSEPH D. LYNCH came up from San Diego, where he had
edited the *Sun* for a year or so. He was of Irish stock, a full-
bodied man weighing from 200 to 225 pounds, of a vigorous
and aggressive temperament and a prolific writer. It was said of
him in San Diego that, if he saw a dog run across the street, he
could write a column editorial about it. What his articles might
have lacked in refinement and profundity they made up in girth.[1]
Lynch was looking for a new and a larger opening, and he fell in
with Col. J. J. Ayers, who was editor of the *Express*. Between
them they arranged a partnership, and purchased the *Express*
from Tiffany & Paynter. They had not made much of a success
of the business because neither Tiffany nor Paynter was a real
newspaper man; but they were just printers with convivial dis-
positions and no aptitude for management. They probably sold
to Ayers & Lynch largely on credit to save themselves from a har-
rying situation. For a brief time under the new ownership the
editorial columns of the *Express* expanded to twice their former
proportions. Then something else happened. The firm of Ayers
& Lynch purchased the *Herald*; perhaps this denouement was

---

[1]Joseph D. Lynch (ca.1833–ca.1907), an Irish Catholic from Pennsylvania, had
been studying for the priesthood when he left school in his teens and took up the
newspaper business in New York. His writing attracted the attention of Thomas Scott,
the railroad magnate, who sent Lynch to San Diego. There he succeeded William Jeff
Gatewood as editor of the San Diego *World*, not the *Sun* as Spalding says. He moved
to Los Angeles in March 1875. *Times*, March 23, 1907. Ayers agreed with Spalding
that Lynch had "fine ability as a writer." *Gold and Sunshine*, p. 271.

in contemplation from the beginning.[2] The Water Company crowd, which had originally purchased the *Herald* in lieu of pressing its libel suit for slandering the service, probably looked upon the property as a doubtful, perhaps a troublesome asset, and was glad to shift the responsibility to other shoulders. The *Herald* was probably sold for a song, and Ayers & Lynch had their own time for singing it. The new status brought about immediate and radical changes. The Spanish and German weekly papers which had been housed and printed by the *Herald* were sent away, and Creighton had to hang his *Republican* hat on a peg elsewhere. Then the *Express* office was moved from across the street, and occupied the vacated space.[3] Mr. Lynch took sole charge of the *Herald*, and Col. Ayers was in command of the *Express*. I was retained on the *Herald* as city editor and the active business man. Mr. Lynch's first demonstration on taking charge was to throw aside the set of double-entry books upon which I had labored so long and faithfully, and substitute a small cash book which he kept on his own desk. All the incoming cash was handed to him, and he kept such track of business matters as suited him in his simpler way. I was not pleased with the way things were moving, but there seemed nothing for me but to hold on as long as my salary continued. I was in debt for my home, and had a wife on my hands, and expectations. So I put my pride in my pocket, repressed my contempt for the pompous, overbearing Irishman in command, and made myself as useful to the establishment as I could. It leaked out, somehow, and got to my ears after a month or two that Lynch observed to somebody "Spalding is a devilish handy man." I certainly endeavored to make myself not simply handy, but indispensable.

The baby was born Sept. 20th, 1876. Aunt Ann had come on from Columbus to be with Mary during the confinement, and in her usually masterful way, took command. I had little to say or do except to employ the physician, Dr. Stanway, and to summon him when the time came. It was arranged that Mrs. Mayo, who was in the house with us still, should act as nurse. Mrs. Mayo had never borne a child herself, and I doubt if she had ever had experience in nursing. The baby was a boy, and seemed to be normal and well-formed, but it lived only ten days. I have always

[2]According to Ayers (*Gold and Sunshine*, p. 271), at this time Lynch alone acquired the *Herald* by lease. The date was Oct. 3, 1876.

[3]"The printing establishment of the *Express* was moved from the second floor of the Temple Block to the quarters of the *Herald*, in the Jones Block on the west side of Spring street opposite the Court House." Spalding, *History*, I, 221.

believed that its death was due to lack of proper care. Let the responsibility rest where it may, the untimely taking off of our first child was a dreadful shock to the mother and myself. I think Aunt Ann felt it keenly also. She had lost her only child when it was a baby, and this revived her own cankering sorrow.[4]

After serving Mr. Lynch as devilish handy man for seven or eight months, his brother Bob came from St. Louis and took my place.[5] I had been with the *Herald* altogether about three years. In this emergency Aunt Ann came to the rescue and advanced sufficient funds to settle with Mr. Beaudry for our home, taking a long time note and mortgage herself. I made a trip to San Francisco to see if I could drum up some advertising for the *Herald* and *Express*, but the expedition did not pan out well. Shortly after my return, Col. Ayers offered me the position of city editor on the *Express*, which I accepted, and settled into a place that suited me much better than my late position on the *Herald*. Col. Ayers was a totally different man, and far more agreeable to work with than Lynch.[6] The sanctums of the two papers were in the afore described little cribs with only a narrow passageway between them. So I had an opportunity to keep tab on my late employer and his brother (who was about as fat and aggressive as himself), and they frequently had a lively tilt, especially when one or the other had "tanked up." I remained on the *Express* about four years and formed a strong personal attachment for Col. Ayers; in fact the friendship endured through the remaining years of his life. During my time of service I was called upon

[4]A poem, "Our Baby Still," has here been omitted. It will be found in Spalding's *Snatches of Song*, p. 155.

The children of William Andrew Spalding (b. Oct. 3, 1852; d. Sept. 7, 1941) and Ellen Mary Dennison Spalding (b. Oct. 10, 1852; d. May 20, 1936) were as follows:

An unnamed son, b. Sept. 20, 1876; d. Sept. 30, 1876.
Hamilton Wood, b. Dec. 30, 1879; d. May 27, 1899.
Jane McCormick, b. Dec. 11, 1881; d. Aug. 4, 1932.
William Dennison, b. May 21, 1883; d. Dec. 18, 1936.
Helen Godfrey, b. Dec. 24, 1885.
Volney Ayers, b. Dec. 29, 1887; d. April 25, 1933.
Thomas Richard, b. Oct. 28, 1889; d. June 24, 1927.
Mary Louise, b. Feb. 22, 1891.

[5]"March 17, 1877: Discharged from the office to give place to Mr. Lynch's brother Robert. Hard times assigned as the cause of the move." Spalding's Diary. In the city and county directory Robert S. Lynch was listed on the *Herald* staff as late as 1883/84.

[6]"July 2d, 1877: Commence work on the *Express* as city editor at a salary of $15 a week. This is not a very large remuneration compared with $35 a week which I formerly got from the *Herald* but I am mighty glad to take it after an enforced leisure of about four months and a half. I like Ayers very much to work with. He is pleasanter in every way than Lynch. Not so insufferably polite and important. I do the local and edit most of the telegraph." Spalding's Diary.

to take full charge of the paper during the Colonel's absence in Sacramento, as a member of the Constitutional Convention, and later, during his campaign for Congress.

One of my makeshifts for enlivening our dull local columns was a resort to pictures. It should be noted that at that time the daily press of the country had not adopted illustration as one of its features. *Harper's Weekly* and *Frank Leslie's* were the only illustrated papers in the country. They were published in New York, and they relied on wood cuts entirely, as modern processes to utilize photography had not been invented.[7] My first effort in that line was a raid on the job office, in which I conscripted the label ring to work into my heading [that] fulminated against the Water Company crowd. My next raid brought a choice array of symbol-cuts—asterisks, moons, suns, stars, and other constellations—with which I illuminated a report of some convivial doings of the local tribe of Red Men.[8] But this trick could not be worked a third time; it would be like repeating a joke on the same audience. Next I secured some type-high boxwood blocks, such as wood-engravings were made upon, and some graver's tools. I had never taken a lesson in drawing, and knew nothing of the graver's art, but went at the task as a rank amateur, one of those fellows who rush in where angels fear to tread. Of course I could not attempt anything in the way of light and shade effects, but I could draw the outline of a simple figure, and cut away the surface of the wood around it, thus producing a silhouette. A series of such cuts was made to illuminate various jingles of a humorous character which were published from time to time to lighten up the columns. My entire accomplishment was comparatively slight, and would not be worth mentioning now were it not for the fact that it was a pioneering gesture in a movement which afterwards grew into great importance, and to-day constitutes one of the established factors of journalism. So, perhaps, as a matter of historical interest, it may be allowable for me to

[7]The first cut in an American newspaper was in 1707, and colonial newspapers frequently used type-metal cuts in connection with their titles. Woodcuts came into use in the 1840's, the New York *Herald* issuing an eight-page pictorial edition of Mexican War scenes. But the process was too slow for timely articles. Frank L. Mott, *American Journalism* (New York, 1941), pp. 44, 294. The real point of Spalding's claim is that he was predating the extensive push toward illustrations that came with Pulitzer and the New York *World* in the 1880's.

[8]The story appeared in the *Express*, Jan. 12, 1878, a clever spoof on a meeting of the fraternal Order of Red Men, probably the Shominac Tribe of Los Angeles, instituted in 1874. In a MS titled "The Beginnings of Newspaper Illustration," in possession of Mrs. Helen Groff, Spalding says he borrowed this idea from John Phoenix, "a noted wit of earlier days, who had worked up a similar stunt on the San Diego *Union*."

resuscitate some of my crude silhouettes, with enough of their accompanying jingles to show the context and excuse for their creation.

"Rime of the Ancient One-eyed Man" was a parody on Coleridge's "Ancient Mariner":

I am constrained by the button-hole, to hear the tale of the ancient Polyphemus.

He holds me by the button-hole:
 "There was a cat," quoth he,
"Oh, shoot the cat, thou one-eyed man,"—
 Said the one-eyed man, "Shoot me,

If I do not to thee unfold
 This wondrous tale of mine;
Thou canst not aye my tale gainsay,
 Nor foil my dark design."

"There was a cat."

He explaineth the nature of the strange interruption.

Upon the moonlit fence without
 A dark'ning figure sat,
And as it lifted up its voice,
 I marked it for a cat.

With Arch-ed Back and Gleaming Eyes.

The ancient man impiously killed the ominous cat.

"God save thee, ancient one-ey'd man,
 From the devils that thee gat"—
"With my boot-jack I hit it whack,
 And killed the loud-voiced cat."

"With my boot-jack I hit it whack—"

And I looked into the night, and lo!
   An hundred leagues in air,
The ghost of the slaughtered cat stood up,
   And it was dancing there.

"The ghost of the slaughtered cat stood up—"

Another one of my skits was entitled "The Wonderful Little Italian Man: A Legend in Verse, Illustrative of Unappreciated Genius and Retributive Justice."

'Tis a curious tale, if the tale be true;
As 'twas told to me, I will tell it to you.

Still another cut introduced some jingle on "Thou Dollar of Our Dad," a take-off for the new trade-dollar recently put forth by the United States Mint.[9]

---

[9]"The Rime of the Ancient One-eyed Man," *Express*, April 27, 1878; "The Wonderful Little Italian Man," *Express*, May 11, 1878; "Thou Dollar of Our Dad," *Express*, June 15, 1878. Spalding forgot, probably because he did not have a clipping of it in his scrapbooks, a slightly earlier poem with five woodcuts, "The Lay of a Jack," signed "Flush Jack," *Express*, March 6, 1878.

Oh, come, thou bright new Dollar.

And one was dedicated to the Owl Dramatic Club, whose amateur performance happened to fall upon a rainy evening.[10]

Dampened, but not Discouraged.

I think this is enough evidence to submit that the Los Angeles *Evening Express* was one of the first newspapers in the country to adopt illustration in its news columns, and that I was the uncelebrated illustrator.[11]

I continued my active service in journalism through the years in which various processes for newspaper illustration were introduced—lithographing, the chalk-plate process, the zinc etching, and finally the photographic half-tone. I took enough interest in these various systems as they came along to make up a line of exhibits, showing each process in its several stages. These I framed, and presented the collection to Gen. H. G. Otis, editor

[10]The Owl Dramatic Club, an outgrowth of activities at the Unitarian Church, gave occasional productions for the city. As Spalding says, regarding the 1870's and 1880's, "For the most part the people of Los Angeles were dependent upon local talent for their entertainment. The Owl Dramatic Club was for them like 'apples of gold in pictures of silver.'" *History*, I, 236-237.

[11]In another manuscript ("Early Struggles in Verse," p. 6; in possession of Mrs. Helen Groff) Spalding makes the more modest claim that his woodcuts were "a first effort on the Los Angeles press to illustrate local news."

of the *Times*. He thought enough of it to hang it on a wall of his sanctum. When the *Times* building was destroyed by dynamite and fire, my exhibit went with the rest.

I have mentioned the enterprise of Prudent Beaudry in opening up his hill lands for settlement—how he was obliged to lay off and grade his own streets and build his own system of water works, and how he eventually built the Temple Street cable railway to give easy access to his "dark domains." All of these developments were tremendously expensive and were not great as revenue producers. He carried a considerable indebtedness, and the sale of lots was not sufficiently rapid or remunerative to meet his burden of interest. About the year 1877 or 1878 Aunt Ann, who had returned to her home in Columbus, Ohio, wrote me that she had sold a piece of property and had $30,000 to loan, asking if I could find a substantial borrower. I suggested Mr. Beaudry, and she, knowing of his standing and enterprising character, consented to loan him the money. Through Fred, his secretary, I had learned that he was in the market for a loan of that amount. The loan was soon negotiated, and I was quite astounded to receive a registered letter containing a draft for $30,000 made in my favor.[12] Aunt Ann must have had considerable confidence in me to put the entire matter in my hands in such summary fashion. However the formalities were closed satisfactorily, and a year or so later, she made another loan of $10,000 to him.

But the times still continued hard, and in a year or so more Beaudry was unable to keep up his interest payments. I was obliged to bring suit to foreclose on the mortgaged property, which included the water works, several houses on Bellevue Avenue, and a tract of about five acres on the edge of the hill facing Charity Street that was in bearing orange and lemon trees. Aunt Ann did not think it advisable to force the matter to a sale in those reactionary times, and so I was appointed a receiver of court to carry on for further developments. And that is how I became manager of the water works, and also a citrus grower on a small scale; also the landlord of several tenements. I performed my functions as receiver in plus of my duties as newsgatherer for the *Express*, employing Andy Lawrence to collect the bills for water service. This arrangement was continued for three or four years, until Mr. Beaudry's brother Victor, a wealthy mining man, came to the rescue, and advanced sufficient funds

[12]According to Spalding's Diary, the money was received on July 8, 1877, at which time the arrangements with Beaudry had already been made.

to take up the obligation, with accrued interest.[13] Meanwhile a sale of the little orange and lemon grove had been effected to a committee of citizens for $10,000, to be donated to the state as a site for the Normal School.[14] The lot was subsequently sold to the city for something over $100,000, and that is where the elegant Public Library stands. So I can claim the honor of having begun my career as an orange-grower on classical ground. When I started as a horticulturist, I sold my crops on the trees to the firm of Woodhead & Gay, the first firm to ship Southern California oranges to the east. The revenue from the orchard just about defrayed the expense of caring for the property.

An episode in connection with my management of the water works is worth recording. The first development of petroleum in Southern California was on; some wells had been bored in the Newhall district, and they were light producers.[15] There was some excitement of a mild sort. Burdette Chandler, a former Pennsylvania man, thought he would like to get into the game, without exactly knowing how.[16] He heard of a well in the western hills that had been sunk by Mr. Beaudry for water, but had been abandoned because oil seeped into it. He got somebody to go down into the well and skim off the thick, tarry residue that remained on top of the water. Then he looked me up and asked if I would experiment with his find, and ascertain if it could be burned in the furnace for the generation of steam. I consented, and he sent several barrels of his gummy asphaltum to the works. Nobody knew anything about burning crude petroleum at that time, and my engineer, named Theobold, tried throwing the sticky mass in with a shovel, but failed to make much headway.

[13]Victor Beaudry, after his merchant days in San Francisco and Nicaragua, had begun his mining career in the San Gabriel area near Los Angeles. His real wealth, however, came when he, along with Mortimer Belshaw, monopolized smelting for the Cerro Gordo mines in Inyo County. Remi A. Nadeau, *City-Makers* (Garden City, N.Y., 1948), p. 38, describes Beaudry as "a French Canadian and a forty-niner, a man of short stature and long mustache, whose natty, well-tailored suits made him a 'dandy' in the midst of Cerro Gordo's uncouth miners."

[14]March 14, 1881, the state legislature provided for the establishment of a branch normal school in Los Angeles. Newmark (p. 532) said that a German, George Gephard, raised eight thousand dollars to purchase the orange grove at Bellevue Terrace near Fifth and Charity streets for a site. The school was opened in 1882, in 1914 moved to Vermont Avenue, and eventually was transformed into the University of California at Los Angeles, now in Westwood.

[15]San Antonio Creek about five miles from Ventura witnessed the first important drilling for oil in southern California in 1865. A small boom followed in the middle 1860's and then a lull. Spalding refers to a second boom which began in the Newhall area about 1876.

[16]Burdette Chandler was a member of the city council, 1880-1882 and 1887-1888.

Finally he came to me and said, "It can't be done. I have thrown it on a bed of live coals, and it put them out." I told Chandler that he could come and get his petroleum. A few years afterwards I learned that Chandler was greatly disgusted at our failure, saying that "Spalding had delayed the development of the petroleum industry in Southern California for years by his stupid course." Which only shows that some ignoramuses expect miracles to tide them over.

A year or so later, however, I did succeed in burning crude petroleum in our furnace. In a trip through the San Gabriel valley I called at the ranch of Gen. George Stoneman, and found he had a newly devised burner that made the liquid fuel available.[17] Inquiry developed the fact that the burner was the invention of Mr. [Milo S.] Baker, of the Baker Iron Works in Los Angeles, and that oil burning had been adopted in that establishment first. I bought a burner from the Baker works, and installed it under the boiler at our plant. It worked satisfactorily, and was a labor-saver. The crude oil was shipped from Newhall, and cost us $1.25 a barrel. Thus, I was the second in the city to adopt crude oil for steam generation, the third in Southern California.

Col. Ayers was in the Constitutional Convention at Sacramento three or four months [1878]. During that time I had entire charge of the paper, writing the editorials, reading proof, and handling the finances. There was a reliable young man in the front office to take care of the details of business, and I also had a news-gatherer to look after local happenings. I took my responsibility very seriously, and being so young at the business, had not acquired the knack of eliminating strain upon myself that older hands enjoy. Business was not any too lively, but I managed to make "one hand wash the other," and pulled the concern through, somehow.

At that time the people of the state were much torn up about political matters. The Southern Pacific machine dominated both of the old political parties. There had been a split-off among those who resented such dictation, and the Workingmen's Party had taken the field in an effort to achieve reform.[18] The *Express* had

[17]General George John Stoneman, a veteran of the Mexican War, was not only a prominent rancher but also a leading political figure in the area.

[18]In a subsequent section, which has been deleted, Spalding wrote: "In the next Congressional campaign [1880] my friend Col. John F. Godfrey received the nomination of the Workingmen's Party. In that campaign I did my first and only political managing. I made a trip through the San Joaquin Valley and arranged for his meetings and obtained the necessary publicity by notices in the papers and handbills. But

been strongly anti-monopoly all through, and had favored the Constitutional Convention as a means of incorporating in the organic law some means of holding railroad and other big corporations in check. Col. Ayers and Gen. Volney E. Howard were elected to the Convention as representatives of the reform movement.[19] They were leaders in the proceedings, and had much to do with adopting the section providing for a Railroad Commission, and other reform measures. In another chapter, under the heading "The Sphinxes of Alameda Street," this matter is referred to in more detail.[20] Suffice it here that the new constitution was looked upon as a triumph for the reform movement, and after a red-hot campaign—with the banks and capitalistic element, and the political machines, and the big lawyers opposed—it was triumphantly carried at the polls. Col. Ayers and Gen. Howard returned to receive the grateful plaudits of their constituents.

For the next state election Col. Ayers was nominated by the Workingmen's Party for Congressman. It was not expected that the split-offs could carry the election, but in the case of Ayers, there were strong hopes that the Democratic Party would indorse the Workingmen's candidate, and thus insure success. Lynch, editor of the *Herald*, and Col. Ayers's business partner, was a delegate to the Democratic Congressional Convention which met at San Luis Obispo, and we looked to him to do all he could to bring about the happy denouement. But when the Convention assembled the railroad influence dominated, and it did not appear that Lynch had a word to say in behalf of his associate. An unprincipled and dissipated lawyer of San Diego, Wallace Leach, was given the Democratic nomination. The Republican Convention nominated Romualdo Pacheco, former Gov-

---

that campaign led to defeat also. The Workingmen's Party was not born under a lucky star."

[19]General Howard, having left San Francisco under duress after his opposition to the idea of vigilance committees, became a leading Los Angeles attorney, specializing in land titles. He was later elected one of the first two superior court judges in Los Angeles County, 1880-1885. William W. Robinson, *Lawyers of Los Angeles* (Los Angeles, 1959), p. 47.

[20]Spalding intended the "Sphinxes" chapter in his *History* (I, 255-259) to be reproduced intact in the "Autobiography." Because it is repetitious, however, and in any case available in print, it has not been included in this edition. The title referred to two bronze figures which graced the terminal of the Los Angeles and Independence Railroad; when the Southern Pacific absorbed the company and demolished its building, the sphinxes mysteriously appeared in the dooryard of the city's notorious prostitute, Cora Phillips. "That was the crowning insult," wrote Spalding, "put upon an outraged community."

ernor of the state, and a complaisant friend of the railroad company."[21]

During the absence of Col. Ayers on his political campaign, I was again in charge of the paper. Naturally I was enthusiastic in his behalf. When the fiasco at San Luis Obispo was pulled off, I felt so outraged that I wrote a rather warm editorial, in which I alluded to the part played by "Judas Iscariot," not mentioning any name, but leaving the public to draw its own inference.[22] This angered Lynch to such an extent that in the *Herald* of the next morning appeared "An Open Letter to One Spalding," in which Lynch poured out the vials of his wrath upon me, using every insulting epithet and insinuation that he could put into print.[23] When I read his outpouring I realized that it meant a

[21]John Steven McGroarty, who knew Wallace Leach, described him as follows: "Dissipated, but industrious, with low instincts, yet not lacking in some admirable traits of character, he was a queer compound of gall and vanity." McGroarty, *Los Angeles: From the Mountains to the Sea* (Chicago, 1921), I, 355.

Romualdo Pacheco (1831-1899) served as a Republican representative in Congress, 1877-1883. He had earlier been a perennial officeholder in the state and acting governor when Governor Newton Booth became a United States senator in 1875.

[22]Spalding's editorial appeared in the *Express*, July 23, 1879, titled "Double-Dyed Treachery." At some length it decried the convention's nomination of Leach, much as Spalding analyzed it above. Toward the end Spalding became, as he said, "warm": "If a more despicable scheme was ever concocted in a Democratic Convention we have not heard of it. Add to the treachery of party principles in general the individual treachery of those who were or should have been the friends of the man sought to be betrayed into the hands of the enemy, and we have a picture which would do justice to Judas Iscariot in the garden of Gethsemane."

[23]*Herald*, Aug. 16, 1879: "Open Letter to One Spalding."
"Sir: For some inscrutable reason, which I shall not attempt to divine, Mr. J. J. Ayers (you must pardon me for not using your invariable toadistic prefix of Honorable before Mr. Ayers's name, a prefix which, in his own paper, as he is not entitled to it by any recognized usage, seems to me indelicate) has placed you in charge of the *Express*, a newspaper which was purchased from the Messrs. Tiffany & Paynter by a company which was organized by my friends. You are a natural puppy and of course you can't forego your natural base instincts. Notwithstanding the desire which I have repeatedly shown to stay out of the present Congressional contest you have again and again tried to interest me by the grossness, grotesqueness and exaggeration of the claims you assert for Mr. Ayers and by your low-lived imputations leveled at me. Mr. Ayers was in no sense entitled to the Democratic nomination for this District. I did not advocate him for that position and I am glad of it. A man who could leave a pismire like you to edit a paper which was intended to advance the interests of an entire community was not entitled to the recognition of a Democratic Convention, even though he were as good a Democrat as he has certainly proved a bad one.
"While you forget that I have some personal interest in the *Express*, which has lately been used as a mere vehicle of Mr. Ayers's ambition, I cannot be equally forgetful. I have had some business relations with you on the *Herald*. When I took charge of this paper I found you on it. At the request of two then friends of yours, whom you have since betrayed, as you will in time betray every one who has anything to do with you, I retained you on the paper at a salary of $40 a week. I found you as expensive a curiosity as ever oppressed the gatherer of a museum. You are naturally of a dog-like and snarling temper and you can make more enemies for a

fight at our first meeting. I knew that he always carried a revolver in his hip pocket, and concluded that he should not have
any advantage of me. So I armed myself, to be fully prepared.
I was standing on the west side of Spring Street nearly in front of
the *Express* office when Lynch came down the sidewalk in front
of Temple Block on the opposite side. When he was just across
the street from me, he sighted me, and began to tug at his hip
pocket. Being a fat man, his pantaloons were probably drawn
tight over his hips, and his revolver must have stuck in his pocket.
At any rate, he danced about considerably in drawing it, and

---

paper in a week than a better mannered and better hearted man could friends in a
month.

"You very well remember that it was less than a week after I took charge of the
Herald when I received a letter under enclosure to me, but which was addressed to
you, from Mr. Bassett, your later employer and the former editor of the *Herald*, tell-
ing you, though doubtless with a view to its effect on me, that you were a dog and a
thief. I treated you with extreme delicacy on that occasion—in fact, as if you had been
a gentleman, a character as foreign to you as it would be to any other tawny cur who
runs Los Angeles streets. While I am not prepared to say that you were a thief, I am
ready to say that I discovered a circumstance in the relation of the principal carrier
of the *Herald* to this office whose rectification—and it should have been rectified by
you as business manager in the interest of the stockholders of the *Herald*—has saved
to this office at least $11 a week in the one hundred and fifty-three weeks during
which I have published the paper. While I do not court the law of libel, and am
therefore technically guarded, Mr. Bassett and myself agree on far more points than
formerly. We especially agree on one point.

"Though a coward by nature and a sneak by intuition and preference, you, about
a year ago, undertook to 'bull-doze' a political meeting. Amongst other things you
left off a list of callers of the meeting the name of a gentleman whose standing in this
community is above reproach, and who, by the way, was one of those who interested
themselves for your retention on the *Herald*. When he asked you why you had taken
such an insulting liberty, you tried to hector and even put your hand on your pistol
pocket. On having your face slapped, you turned and ran like a scared hound. In your
cowardly confusion and terror you encountered the iron chain which connects the
posts in front of the Court House, and your impetus was so violent and your heels so
nimble that you turned a double somersault over this physical impediment. You then,
with the sagacity of fear and the impulse of terror crowded your miserable, palpi-
tating carcass into the narrow space which separates the Capitol store from Dr.
Shorb's office. Since then, with the view of denying refuge to cowards, this passage-
way has been boarded up. With a forbearance which you would never show to any
one, the *Herald* forebore all mention of this shameful episode. Since then you have
been as safe as any woman from a man's notice.

"Hereafter I shall discuss Col. Ayer's candidacy with as much freedom as I would
any one else's. You have had the insolence—an insolence not rebuked by him—to intimate treachery upon my part to him. You have painted me as a Judas Iscariot and
held me responsible for the failure of a Democratic Convention to nominate Mr.
Ayers for Congress. The fact is that no one in that body desired to nominate Col.
Ayers and I would have been powerless to influence it one way or the other. Your allu-
sion to Judas Iscariot was an unfortunate one. Whatever may be my avoirdupois, good
faith and 'squareness' are written on my face. As for you, you are the very beau
ideal of a physical reproduction of Judas Iscariot. You have the downlook and the
pusillanimous expression of a betrayer who would lack the courage to hang himself
in a moment of remorse. Yours truly,   Joseph D. Lynch."

meanwhile I brought my gun into action. The testimony of witnesses was that he made the first motion to draw, but that I fired the first shot. I was using a short "Bull-dog," self-cocking revolver, a notoriously inaccurate weapon, and had never practiced at shooting. Naturally my shots went wild. Lynch finally got his gun limbered up and fired two or three shots at me, which were equally ineffective. He jumped behind a barber's pole to fire his last shot, and then he ducked into Fred Dohs's barber shop. As I continued to fire I advanced, and when the fracas was over I was standing in the middle of the street, and he was in the barber shop. Constable [R. A.] Ling came up to me and demanded my weapon, which I gave him, and he placed me under arrest. He merely took me to my own office, however, and I was not put to the humiliation of being escorted to the Sheriff's office or to jail. Later I gave bond for my appearance when required.

Of course there was considerable excitement in the old town over the shooting. But everybody understood just why it had taken place. Afterwards I was indicted and stood trial. My good friend Col. John F. Godfrey volunteered to defend me without charge.[24] Judge R. M. Widney made a similar offer. I accepted the tender of Col. Godfrey, and at his suggestion, employed Stephen M. White as associate counsel, paying therefor $100.[25] The trial was not long or involved; the evidence was clear, as stated above, and my lawyers made such a good showing against a rather weak prosecution, that the jury found short work of it, and on the first ballot (which required only about ten minutes) returned a verdict of not guilty.

[24]John Franklin Godfrey (1839-1885), son of an Abolitionist editor, had gone to sea from Maine and landed in South America where he raised sheep. Returning to the United States to fight in the Civil War, he later scouted with the army in the West. He then settled down in Maine, studying law and marrying. For his wife's health he came to Los Angeles in 1874. He was elected city attorney on the People's ticket (1876-1880), served in the Constitutional Convention, and was consistently involved with third parties like the Workingmen's Party or the Greenback-Labor Party.

Spalding considered Godfrey one of his closest friends, in 1885 naming his second daughter, Helen Godfrey (now Mrs. Gregory Groff), after him and delivering a moving tribute to the man before the John F. Godfrey Post of the G. A. R. in Pasadena, Dec. 22, 1892. In this speech he referred to Godfrey as "too independent, too outspoken—too much of an enemy to the shams and abuses of politics—too bitter an opponent of monopolistic influences which then dominated the State—to make a very successful politician." And again, "Just like a woman, and yet such a manly man! He could not look unmoved upon distress, even in the simulation of the stage. A great, big, tender-hearted hero!" Spalding Papers, Huntington Library.

[25]Stephen Mallory White (1853-1901), a native of San Francisco who moved to Los Angeles in 1874, served in the state Senate, 1886-1890, and the national Senate, 1893-1899. He was especially remembered for the zeal with which he successfully fought against Collis P. Huntington for San Pedro as the Los Angeles harbor.

I am not going to venture on any moral homily on my conduct in this affair, preferring to leave it on the bare statement of facts. I think, however, I was glad afterwards that I did not hit Lynch, and of course I was glad he did not hit me. One bystander, named [L. A.] Majors [of Compton], was struck on the thigh by a glancing ball, supposed to have been one of mine, but the impact was not sufficient to break the skin. I looked him up the next day and apologized and gave him a twenty dollar gold piece. He seemed entirely satisfied, and was my friend thenceforward. He probably would have been willing to take another black-and-blue spot at the same price. Col. Ayers came home as soon as he heard of the fracas. When I met him at the station his first words were, "Why didn't you kill the damned scoundrel?"[26]

[26]About 1907 Spalding wrote a ten-page piece called "My 'Scrap' with Lynch" (Spalding Papers, Huntington Library), justifying for the sake of his children his action in the case. Most of the details are repetitious; he begins, however, with a paragraph which would indicate the matter was still important to him at that later time:

"My enemy is dead. The man whose life I once attempted to take and who in turn attempted to take mine, has gone to his final accounting. Were I a believer in the Catholic faith, as he was, I would contribute something to a priest to pray his soul out of purgatory. Let this be taken as an evidence that my animosities do not extend beyond the grave." Later Spalding refers to the Lynch editorial, "To One Spalding," as "the most vilely abusive, the most gratuitous, the most malicious of anything that I have ever seen in print. . . . it was as strong as a hot Irish temper, supported by a masterful command of the English language could make it.

"Now, what was I to do in the face of this situation? Lynch . . . was a man ten years my senior, weighing probably 250 pounds, large of frame, muscular and a bully. My weight was about 145 lbs., and I was run down, nearly to the point of nervous collapse (as it afterwards proved) by over work. To go to him quietly and in a reasonable way and ask a retraction would have resulted in my final humiliation by being thrashed and kicked out of his office. To have recourse to the law, by beginning a libel suit, would have been regarded by the community as the shallowest subterfuge to cover my cowardice. To retort, in kind, through the columns of the *Express* would have been to open a campaign of billingsgate and vituperation against which my soul revolted.

"I was a high-strung young fellow of twenty-eight; had a young wife and the finest baby boy in the world; had lived in the town about six years and felt rather proud of a position which had been attained by the hardest kind of work. I was not ready to resign all this on such an onslaught and sneak away like a coward, or remain under the contempt of the community, to be slowly elbowed out."

Spalding lists the witnesses to the fracas as Henry T. Gage, Isaac W. Lord, Peter Curran, R. A. Ling, and L. A. Majors.

The Spalding-Lynch feud was symptomatic of contemporary journalistic tempers. Spalding remembered from his Kansas City days the assassination of the *Journal's* editor, Col. John Wilder. Later on, at least one other newspaperman, Charles De Young of the San Francisco *Chronicle*, was involved in a shooting under circumstances somewhat similar to those of the Spalding-Lynch duel. Hubert Howe Bancroft, *History of California* (San Francisco, 1886-1890), VII, 400n. And early in 1884 the printer T. S. Harris was sentenced to San Quentin for his shooting of Charles Whitehead, editor of the Los Angeles *Evening Republican*. Spalding, *History*, I, 251. This Harris is not to be confused with S. T. Harris, a printer in whose home Spalding and Fred Wood had lived briefly in the seventies. T. S. Harris did not come to Los Angeles until 1881.

Chapter VIII

POLITICS AND THE BOOM
(1874-1881)

I T MAY OCCUR to some that, in describing the early business
establishments of Los Angeles, I have put an undue emphasis
on the saloons. But, if an accurate picture of the old town is
to be drawn, they cannot be minimized or ignored. The saloon
men really cut a good deal of ice—and dispensed it too. Everything was "wide open" in those days, and I do not remember any
ordinance requiring screens in front of bars either. People were
not so squeamish about taking a drink, or seeing somebody else
take one. It was like Kipling's Mandalay, "Where the best is like
the worst, [. . .] and a man can raise a thirst"—and satisfy it
also, without any great to-do being made about it. Such of the
saloons as elected to do so kept open all night, and all elected to
keep open on Sunday; in fact that was the day when their patrons
had the most time at their disposal, and felt in the most mellow-
ing mood.[1]

[1]Charles D. Willard, *The Herald's History of Los Angeles City* (Los Angeles,
1901), p. 320, says that in 1870 there were 110 saloons for a population of 5,000.

Spalding described the Palace Saloon in the Temple Block about 1874 as "the most
elegant institution in town. The front was finished in white enamel, with curved
plate-glass windows on each side of the impressive entrance. The inside of the place
was also finished in white enamel, the walls and ceiling elaborately paneled. The bar
was of the same finish in front, and the sideboard, of striking design, with its array of
cut-glass bowls, decanters, and shining tumblers, goblets and glasses of every con-

The first drive for something more high-toned came when the churches and the better class of citizens made common cause for Sunday closing. The progressive newspapers helped the cause, and, after several successive campaigns, a council was elected pledged to take steps in the matter, and a Sunday closing ordinance was adopted and put into effect.[2] It went hard with some people who had for years enjoyed their vested right of Sunday boozing; the saloon men said that their business was going to be ruined, and there was much talk of the iniquity and hardship of sumptuary laws; but after all, things went on much the same as before, only they were a little more decent on Sundays. Whether the church attendance was much augmented is doubtful; it would require statistics to prove it. But at first there was a good deal of covert evasion of the Sunday law, just as there is a good deal of boot-legging now-a-days. I remember a funny incident. There was a fellow named Weiss, a German shoe-maker, whom everybody knew, because of a certain peculiarity.[3] He was a rather fine figure of a man, tall and straight, shoulders back, like all who had early military training in Germany, and he was not a bad boozer at all, only he had kept up one of his German traditions of taking his "schnapps," first thing in the morning. If he did not get his "schnapps," the day did not start off right and was apt to prove a blank failure. Weiss's peculiarity was that his voice had broken in youth, and he talked in a falsetto. Coming from so robust and soldierly a man, the effect was very striking. His ordinary talk was trying enough on the risibles, but when he got excited or emphatic, and stressed a final syllable, his voice went up into a wail that was truly heart-rending. No decent man ever laughed at his infirmity before him—it must have been

ceivable design, was a work of art. There were some oil paintings of chaste and elegant execution . . . . But the master-piece was a chandelier that hung from the middle of the ceiling. This was decorated with countless prismatic glass pendants that glinted the lights in a way that was dazzling." *History,* I, 199-200.

2"In this year [1874] a lively campaign was waged for license and control of the saloon business. The Good Templars and extreme prohibitionists refused to support the reform measure on the ground that they could not countenance a compromise with sin; consequently they and the saloon people voted against the measure. But there were enough level-headed voters to carry the reform by a good majority, and, for the first time in its history, Los Angeles placed a limit on the number of saloons to be allowed, and subjected them to pretty stiff regulations, among which was that they should be closed on Sunday." Spalding, *History,* I, 210.

3The directory of 1875 lists A. Weiss, a boot- and shoemaker, residing at the corner of First and Main.

mortifying enough, even when seemingly ignored—and those who knew him best and saw most of him finally got so that they hardly noticed it [at] all; it was just a matter of course. The first Sunday morning after the closing ordinance went into effect Weiss sauntered down town, as usual, and when he reached his accustomed place, was surprised to find the door locked and the shutters up. He had forgotten about the sumptuary legislation, and had made no provision against it. But the situation dawned on him after a moment of thought, and he was in a panic. Walking down street with a very dejected air, he encountered an old friend, Ollie Huckett, standing at the corner of an alley. *"Ollie,"* he said, in his real earnest falsetto, *"do you know where a fellow can get a drink?"*

Ollie sized up the predicament, and without making light of it, directed Weiss down the alley, through a little court on that side, the door on the left; knock three times, slow.

Weiss followed directions and disappeared. Ollie was waiting for somebody who was slow in keeping an appointment, and remained at the corner of the alley. In about five minutes Weiss came out, looking much more hopeful, and wiping his lips.

"Ollie," he shrieked, *"you . . . have . . . . saved . . . my . . li-i-i-i-f-e!"*

After Sunday-closing had been in force some time, it occurred to somebody that it would be a good thing to close the saloons on election days also. There had come to be a good deal of drunkenness and rowdyism on such occasions, and sometimes infractions of the peace at the very polls. That time it was not so difficult to push the reform through, for the politicians had come to realize that it was worth while to listen to the better elements of the town when they demanded something. But election-day closing was occasionally dodged.[4]

[HOW MR. PIPER VOTED

And the Remarkable Incidents that Befell him on his Way Down Town to do it—Also How a Righteous Law is Rigidly Maintained.

When Mr. Piper sauntered down town yesterday morning he was athirst. A sensation of uncompromising dryness pervaded his throat which would not down. . . . As he approached the familiar place of cheer, he found to his astonishment that the front shutters were up, the door locked and the banquet hall deserted. . . .

[4]The following story was at one time intended by Spalding to be inserted here. Selections have been excerpted by the editor from the *Express*, Oct. 18, 1877.

He stood for a moment silently contemplating the blank, uninviting front and then turned sorrowfully away.

"Well, I suppose I must go and patronize the other place," and he crossed the street.

But the other place was closed and barred too.

"I say, my friend," said Mr. Piper, hailing a passer-by, "Anything happened?—panic?—riot?—insurrection?" . . .

"Election-day," replied the other.

"By gum! so it is," exclaimed Mr. Piper; "I never thought of that."

Then our friend started moodily on his way down street again, the hard, dry lump in his throat getting harder and drier with every step.

"Darn such a law," he pettishly ejaculated; "I say darn such an un-republican, un-democratic law which won't let a man vote and take a drink of whisky in the same day."

Now, Mr. Piper was possessed of the general characteristic of human nature: If a thing was denied him, he wanted it just so much the more; if it was positively forbidden, then he *must* have it at all hazards. . . .

As he walked along, revolving these things in his mind, he bethought him of a subterfuge. Approaching a special officer, stationed at the corner, with a very military aspect (having a pair of shoulder braces on for the occasion and a big badge attached to the lappel of his coat) Mr. Piper accosted him in a friendly manner.

The officer responded with the dignity and reserve which his exalted position required.

"My friend," said Mr. Piper, reaching out and placing a quarter in the hand of the officer, "I'm dry."

The special looked him in the eye for half a second, at the same time executing a series of winks—two with the left eye, one with the right and then two more with the left.

"Yes," said Mr. Piper.

"All right, come with me," responded the guardian of the peace.

He led the way through a tailor shop, into a little back yard where a charcoal fire was cooking an iron goose, preparatory for application to the new made pants. They climbed upon a pile of dry-good boxes, over a high board fence, to the roof of a wood-shed on the other side, and thence dropped to the ground in the next yard.

"Mum's the word," said the officer, re arranging his disorded suspenders, and they stepped into the rear door of a saloon which had its front shutters up.

The saloon keeper was there, arrayed in his guady white vest and clean apron, much as usual, smiling and gracious.

"This gent'l'm'n and me," said the special, "wants a little cold tea." . . .

The saloon man seemed to comprehend. Would they have it straight?

"A little ginger'n pep'mint in mine, if you please," said the officer, "I always take the seasonin' with my tea."

Mr. Piper preferred his with water and sugar.

The saloon man prepared the glasses and poured the harmless beverage out of a black bottle with a long neck. Being invited to participate, he also took some himself.

When the glasses had been tipped and drained, the Special excused himself on the line of attending to duty, and gracefully bowed himself out of the back door, while Mr. Piper laid down half a dollar to cover the expense of the tea.

"That's easy enough done" thought Mr. Piper to himself, as he retraced his steps and gained the street once more, feeling much exhilarated. "I wonder whether all the saloons do that; what a bully way to get around the law though, he, he, he!" and he chuckled with lively satisfaction.

By this time he had arrived in front of another gloomy looking place of beverage, quiet as the grave.

"Now I'll try this one, just for luck, he thought, and then I'll go down and vote."

With less difficulty than in the previous instance he found his way to the rear of the establishment, and, sure enough, the back door was ajar. Here he did the cold tea a second time, and, a friend, dropping in at the back door just as he was about to leave, he accepted a pressing invitation to indulge again.

"Now," said Mr. Piper, "I must go down and vote." . . .

Mr. Piper started off by a circuitous route to deposit his ballot. Just how many more shams in the ostensibly closed saloons he exposed, we are not prepared to state. We are convinced, however, that he held to his original resolution to drink cold tea at them all.]

Some years later, when another campaign was instituted to establish high license [fees], strict regulation and a limitation of the number of saloons to be allowed, a peculiar situation was developed. The ultra prohibitionists took high ground against "licensing sin," and opposed the measure. Nothing would satisfy them but to "pulverize the rum power" then and there. The saloons and all the influences that were on their side also fought fiercely against the high license measure. Thus we found the extreme prohibitionists and the saloon element fighting side by side to defeat a most valuable reform.[5] Fortunately the common-sense element of the community was in a majority against the strange combination, and high license carried. That was the beginning of the downfall of the saloon influence in politics. Before that it had insidiously asserted itself through one political party or another, and, by shifting its weight, had generally turned the result to suit its own purpose. But, with high license and strict

[5]In his *History* Spalding described a similar coalition in the earlier 1874 campaign. See this chapter, n. 2. These circumstances probably prevailed in both instances.

regulation, it learned to keep its hands out of politics. That re-form paved the way for prohibition, which came so recently. The first important step had to be taken against the strenuous opposition of the prohibitionists, as well as that of "the rum power."

In those days little account was taken of sea-side resorts. Some people had a fancy for going down to the mouth of Santa Monica canyon, and camping just above the shingly bed under the old sycamores, for a picnic outing of a day or two, or a week. There was a spring in the canyon that furnished good water, and I believe that in the season Will Tell or some other publican kept open a little shack from which he furnished camping provisions, beer and wine.[6] There was no such thing as a bathing house, however, and whether the campers generally availed themselves of the facilities pure and simple of taking an occasional dip in the surf, I do not know. One occasion, however—not of a trip to Santa Monica, but to the lagoon now called Balboa—is strongly impressed on my mind. We did not call it Balboa then, but it was referred to as the Lagoon, or "Will Tell's," or "the Salt Works"— there having been at some previous time a salt-reducing plant at or near the lagoon.[7] The place was resorted to more for duck hunting than for anything else, and during the season Will Tell kept a depot for supplies and liquidation such as referred to at the canyon. One time a small crowd—our set—arranged a little excursion to Will Tell's for the sake of a novel experience, and to spy out the land. We found Will Tell, a good-natured and rather elderly German, in the field of his greatest usefulness, and a few purchases of crackers, cheese and herring, possibly a bottle or two of beer, as well, put us in good standing with our host. There were no other people at the resort except a party of young men and girls who were paddling up and down the lagoon in a boat no doubt hired from Tell, and they seemed to be having a very jolly time. In default of anything else to do for amusement, we thought of taking a dip in the surf, outside the lagoon. So we asked our host if he could accommodate us with some overalls

[6]There seems to be no evidence that Will Tell ever had a store in Santa Monica Canyon, although he is known to have had establishments at Ballona and in Santa Monica at Fourth Street and Utah Avenue.

[7]Spalding has here confused Balboa with the Ballona lagoon. One story of a day at Will Tell's, which may have been Spalding's, appeared in the *Herald*, July 29, 1874. Ayers (*Gold and Sunshine*, p. 265) said, "it was very much the fashion amongst the 'four hundred' of that period [the early 1870's] to take a 'spin' down to Tell's behind a fast team and enjoy the luxury of a fine dinner."

or pantaloons—any old things that would not be injured by the wetting—so that we could go in. "You don't need id," he said. "You yust go the odder side of dot leedle sand-hill, and take off your clodes, and go ahead. If dose young peebles come aroundt, dey'll go away agin." His reasoning seemed logical, so we adopted the suggestion. On the "odder side," as innocent as so many September Morns, we had our first bout with old Neptune, and formed an intimate acquaintance with the great Pacific Ocean which was the source of much pleasure in after years. No bath ever taken subsequently, however, gave more satisfaction, or had more of the true spirit of adventure in it than that.

Mention has been made of Don Mateo Keller's early booming operations in opening his Aliso Street tract, and of Prudent Beaudry's heroic struggle to make the hill section habitable. There were other subdivisions which found more or less encouragement, but nothing very spontaneous developed in those early movements. For be it remembered, the events now discussed were long before the first big boom arrived in the middle and latter eighties. Most notable among those preliminary subdivisions was Gov. Downey's tract, west of Hill Street and south of Seventh.[8] Although Don Mateo had rather vaguely referred to it as "Downey's dark domain," it was not so very dark, although considered pretty well out in the southwestern suburbs. There were conservative people in the old town who could not see how the city was ever going to wander out so far, and by such the Governor was regarded as a visionary. Besides, if the place should spread, why not on the moist and fertile lands along the river, where a man could grow something? To the southwest everything was bare and forbidding most of the year, and there was no water for irrigation, for the woolen mill ditch was not yet even projected. If anybody had suggested making the country green by using domestic water from the pipes, he would have been considered a worse visionary than the Governor himself. No, it was "the Equerry side" that held out the more inviting prospect those days, and when Don Mateo brought into his advertisement that

[8]John Gately Downey, an Irish druggist, came to Los Angeles in 1850, twice sat on the city council in the 1850's, and in 1860 became the first state governor from southern California. Spalding described him as "a man of medium height and fairly rotund form, with full whiskers, trimmed moderately short, and always a benignant, placid appearance, and a most kindly address when one engaged him in conversation." He once recited to Spalding one of Downey's own articles. "After reading a particularly well rounded period or two, he would pause and ask, 'Now, isn't that illegant language?'" Spalding, *History*, I, 241.

gag about "what fine legs your master has," he perpetrated an Irish witticism that everybody could appreciate; he was referring to the magnificent distance which one would have to travel in reaching the "dark domains" of Downey and Beaudry, even provided they opened a street to "let the light shine in."

Another early tract that excited interest was W. H. Workman's Boyle Heights, named for his father-in-law, Col. Boyle.[9] The East Side tract, laid off by Dr. John S. Griffin, was also a candidate for settlement, although it was considerably isolated by being across the river from the main town, and [there was] only a temporary walk of planks over the stream. It was safe enough in ordinary times, but at high water in the rainy season, the bridge did not exist. Dr. Griffin had received a tract of a thousand acres or so from the city as compensation for his services, acting as health officer during one of the early small-pox epidemics [1863]. The town was too poor to pay money; hence the compromise.[10]

The Morris Vineyard tract on Main Street, west side, north of Washington, came in some time later.[11] It was a piece of perhaps twenty acres, in bearing vines, with a little square adobe house on the Main Street side, which was said to have been the headquarters of Gen. Fremont during his brief season of sojourn in Los Angeles, after his famous pathfinding trip. This tradition was probably unfounded.[12]

An early booming enterprise that I happened to have a hand in was Brooklyn Heights. A company was made up with A. H. Judson of the abstract firm of Judson & Gillette as its president, and Gillette, Frank Gibson, Andy Lawrence, George Safford,

[9]William Henry Workman, from a large Los Angeles family, was a ubiquitous city councilman (serving all but two of the years between 1872 and 1880) and was elected mayor in 1887. His father-in-law, Andrew A. Boyle, a shoemaker, came to Los Angeles in 1858 and planted grapes on the tract later given his name.

[10]John Strother Griffin settled in Los Angeles in 1854 after serving as surgeon under Kearny in the conquest of California. He became one of the city's leading doctors, was superintendent of schools in 1856-1857, was city councilman in 1858-1859, and until the end of the century was generally active in water development, subdivision, and other civic affairs.

[11]Newmark (p. 104) remembered the gracious hospitality dispensed by Moritz Morris and his family from their house in the vineyard between what is now Main, Hill, Fifteenth, and Sixteenth streets. Morris was city councilman, 1866-1870.

[12]Joseph Gregg Layne, *Annals of Los Angeles* (San Francisco, 1935), p. 44, calls the Morris adobe the "most persistent of these Frémont headquarters fakes." The only headquarters that Frémont ever had in Los Angeles was the Alexander Bell home on the corner of Aliso and Los Angeles streets.

McAllister and others of our acquaintance were in it.[13] On the rolling hills east of the river we bought from M. Morris a tract of one hundred acres at $100 an acre. After acquiring the land we found we had no opening to the main thoroughfare, Aliso Street, so we dickered with W. H. Perry for a triangular piece of about an acre that would let us in and out. Perry owned several acres, upon which he had built a fine house for his own residence. He made us pay $600 for the odd piece, and we thought he "put it to us" pretty stiff. However, after taking enough for a roadway, we sold the remainder of the lot to the city for school purposes, price $1,000, and a little wooden building was erected. Perry didn't like that very much, alongside his fine house, but we were rather pleased by the outcome.[14] However, after providing an ample approach, and platting the land in most attractive fashion, we found there was no great rush for our lots. There was some talk of trying to make good on the venture by turning the tract into a cemetery; if we could not get live people, we might be satisfied with the dead. But it was finally decided that the property was too near the main part of town for burial purposes. About that time I sold my interest for a little more than I had put in, and counted myself lucky to get out of the scrape. But other members of the company, with some accessions, formed a new syndicate, and purchased another tract a mile or two further east, where they proceeded to lay off and establish Evergreen Cemetery. In order to gain something in the way of official recognition, they assigned an acre or two on the lower part of the land for a potters' field, and for that tendered a deed to the city as a gift. There developed in the council a lively opposition to its acceptance. The principal reason urged by the objectors was that they did not want to encourage private speculation in the matter of furnishing places of burial. At that time there was no cemetery except the old one on Fort Hill, and that was so nearly filled it was evident something would have to be

[13]"The pioneer in the 'certificate of title' field in Los Angeles was Albert H. Judson, a real-estate-minded lawyer who had been admitted to the New York bar in 1861 and who came to Los Angeles in 1873. At least as early as January of 1875 certificates of title were being issued from the 'Office of Judson and Gillette—Examiners of Title,' the last named being County Recorder J. W. Gillette." Robinson, *Lawyers*, p. 54.

McAllister was a close friend of Spalding; he appears earlier at the Alden Drier banquet; but even in Spalding's Diary he is never given any other first name than "Mac."

[14]William Hayes Perry was a carpenter who, after he came to Los Angeles in 1854, turned furniture maker and married into the Dalton family. His investments in real estate proved profitable, as did his organization in the 1860's of the Los Angeles Gas Company. He was a city councilman during much of this period.

done before long to provide for public requirements. Yet the council proposed nothing to meet the situation. In due time the deed was submitted to the council, accompanied by an ordinance accepting it, and allowing burials in the new cemetery. The lot was accepted by a vote of five to four; but when it came to the ordinance, there were not enough to adopt it, the requirement being seven. While the opposition were glowing with the defeat of the measure, Judge Thompson stepped to the clerk's desk, took the paper, crossed out the words "Be it enacted," and substituted the words "Be it resolved," offering it then as a resolution. This raised a tremendous storm. The rest of the proceedings are graphically reported as follows:

Mr. Cohn—(growing purple in the face) Mr. President, I protest against taking snap judgment against us in this way. I protest! I protest! Mr. Clerk, enter this in full on your minutes!

Mr. Leahy—(springing to his feet and gesticulating like a Halladay windmill) Mr. Mayor, that's the identical thing we voted down two minutes ago. Enter my protest too, Mr. Clerk! Do you want to put your dead in the hands of a monopoly? No Sir; when a man's family dies, he wants them all buried in the same hole! (Sensation in the lobby.)

Mr. Potts—(also a little excited) Mr. President, I can't see why these men object to a-having a grave yard the other side of the river for. I should rejoice to bury my family over there; I should rejoice to bury myself there (laughter in the lobby)— that is, when I die. (Renewed laughter.)

Mr. Cohn—This is a monopoly of the worst kind, and you can't keep them from imposing on the people. By and by they'll sell out to some such man as little Potts here, and then he'll say "Now you —— pay." He's just the man to do it! (Mr. Cohn was called to order.)

Mr. Workman moved to lay on the table one week. Lost.

Mr. Kuhrts wanted his protest entered.

The vote on Mr. Thompson's resolution was then called: Ayes —Thompson, Green, Potts, Waldron and Sotello. (Cohn, Kuhrts, Workman and Leahy refused to vote.) Carried.[15]

And so the potters' field in Evergreen became city property, and so remains to this day, and in more than one sense, is "as broad as it is long." Looking at the matter from this distance, however, it seems to me that Mr. Cohn and the other conscien-

[15]Spalding's account of these proceedings appeared in the *Express*, Aug. 24, 1877. He has quoted it here almost, but not quite, verbatim. Earlier discussions of the cemetery appeared in the *Express*, July 9 and 10, 1877.

tious objectors were fundamentally right. A place of burial ought not to be a matter of private exploitation. If the old council had shown the foresight to appropriate a large block of land some where in the suburbs, order it parked, and open it to the public for a cemetery, lots to be sold for enough to cover maintenance of the place, what a vast amount of money might have been saved for the community in subsequent years. But the council did not have that foresight, and it is doubtful if the public would have sustained them in such a wild venture.

After the birth and untimely death of our first child the Mayos remained with us in our cottage on the hill only a short time. Aunt Ann had come to live with us for an indefinite period, and we probably needed the entire house. We parted with the Mayos on good terms, and maintained friendship with them as long as they remained in Los Angeles.

Our second son was born Dec. 30th, 1879. We called him Hamilton Wood, the first name after Aunt Ann, who had been a fairy Godmother to us, and the second as a tribute to my chum of long standing, Fred Wood.

Col. Ayers was not elected to Congress, but he brought back from his campaign something worse than his defeat. In former years he had been the victim of an insatiate appetite for liquor. On coming to Los Angeles to edit the *Express*, he had broken off the habit of periodical sprees, and for years he was a strict teetotaler, and an honored member of Merrill Lodge, Good Templars. But the political campaigning threw him down from his pedestal. He did not degenerate into a regular soak, but semi-occasionally got started on a jamboree that would last from three or four days or a week, and leave him a sick man for several days afterward. These carnivals were especially hard on me, as the entire burden of getting out the paper was shifted to my hands without preliminary notice. If he failed to be at his desk by ten o'clock any morning, I knew what was required of me. That was to supply the news columns as usual, write the editorials, read all the proof, and carry all the burdens. That was entirely too much for one man to undertake, and of course the work had to go "with a lick and a promise." One thing that made it worse was that about noon Mrs. Ayers would swoop into the office with the inquiry "Have ye seen aneything of Jim?" Mrs. Ayers was a full-bodied person with hair even lighter than straw color, and pink eyes—a veritable Albino. She had the brogue and the manners of an Irish Biddy. How the Colonel ever came to marry a person so far from his own cultural standard was an enigma to his friends. I was told, by way of gossip, that he married her in one of his sprees before coming to Los Angeles, and that was the only explanation that seemed reasonable to me.

About the time of her appearance I would be in the thick of my troubles, and could only take time to tell her that I had not seen Jim, but as soon as I got the paper off my hands, I would look for him, and if possible, get him home. That meant that, as soon as the last proof had been handed in, and the issue of the paper made sure, I had to sally forth in a canvass of the saloons to locate my boss and try to induce him to go home. After the Colonel had exhausted himself in one of his sprees, and recovered from the subsequent prostration, he would be at his desk again, entirely normal and with all of his accustomed dignity. And, somehow, he retained the respect and confidence of the community, and under his conscientious and able editorship, the *Express* was by long odds the most influential newspaper in Southern California.

In those pioneer times people were accustomed to make allowance for the idiosyncrasies cf their great men. At the next State election Col. Ayers through his editorial columns actually picked out the Governor. At an early date he suggested Gen. George Stoneman for that position, and by consistent support kept his name before the public. Gen. Stoneman had served on the recently constituted Railroad Commission and had stood staunchly for the interests of the people, while both of his colleagues had fallen down to the railroad influence. That made the General a marked man, and his nomination for the chief executive of the state was both timely and popular. He was duly nominated and elected.[16] After his installation he acknowledged his indebtedness to Col. Ayers by appointing him to the position of State Printer. When he assumed these grave responsibilities at Sacramento I think the Colonel again went on the water wagon, and he gave a good, conscientious administration of the office. It was during his term that the state assumed the responsibility of printing the text books for the public schools. But, before going to Sacramento, Col. Ayers divorced the Albino woman. He may have had good reason for doing so, outside the fact of general incongruity. In an unusual burst of confidence to me one time he said, "She kept the bottle before me all the time."[17]

[16]George John Stoneman served as governor from 1883 to 1887.

[17]"During Col. Ayers' administration of the State Printing Office, he paid court to and married Miss Charlotte Slater, a daughter of one of the pioneer families, a woman of mature years, refined, and with a fund of common-sense that made her a fit com-

I had something to do indirectly in helping Gen. Stoneman make his campaign. Shortly after his nomination, knowing that he was in rather close circumstances, I asked if he needed financial assistance to make his campaign. He said he did. I procured a loan of $1,000 for him from Aunt Ann. Thus he was able to keep clear of the political cabals who would have been glad to finance him with a string or two attached. I did not ask any political favor from him. Aunt Ann was repaid a couple of years later.

But, while all this was taking place, my health was giving way. I had been on a long strain while the Colonel was in the Constitutional Convention; this was followed by the strain when he was away campaigning, and the episode with Lynch. After the failure of the Congressional campaign, I was again subjected to the intolerable strain of the Colonel's idiosyncrasies. The little den in which I had to do this work was illy lighted, cramped and unsanitary. First my eyes began to give trouble, and then my nerves showed general demoralization. I could not get to sleep until late in the night, and then only by the aid of a cold compress on the back of my head and neck. I must have been close to a complete break-down. I realized that I must make a quick and radical change in my habits of life or Mary would soon be a widow. Naturally I thought of and longed for the great open spaces. My friend N. C. Carter, the excursionist, was about to put a new tract on the market.[18] He had purchased from Lucky Baldwin eleven hundred acres, on the foothills just north of Santa Anita ranch, and proceeded to develop a water system, and lay it off in forty-acre lots, which he offered for sale under the title of the Sierra Madre Tract. That suited my fancy exactly, and Carter agreed to let me in on the "ground floor." I purchased a forty-acre piece near the middle of the tract, for which I agreed to pay Carter $50 an acre. A small payment was made, and the balance was

---

panion for him. The marriage took place May 12th, 1884. In 1886, when Col. Ayers was on a visit to Los Angeles, he quite overcame me by the presentation of a valuable Howard watch in gold case and a heavy gold chain attached. On the inner leaf it bears this inscription: 'James J. Ayers to W. A. Spalding, In token of Loyalty to duty and Friendship. Feb. 18th, 1886.'" This paragraph is part of a section deleted from the end of this chapter.

Late in 1886 Ayers returned to Los Angeles and bought a half interest in the *Herald*, the other owner being Joseph Lynch.

[18]Nathaniel C. Carter had earlier developed land near San Gabriel which, after extensive advertising, he settled with New Englanders. After 1874 his Carter excursions brought trainloads of people to Los Angeles.

on long time and easy installments. And that is how and why, after a service of about seven years in newspapering I became a farmer.[19]

[19]At this point in the "Autobiography" Spalding intended four chapters to be reproduced intact from his *History*, I: "Street Scenes in Old Los Angeles" (pp. 238-244), "Odd Characters of Old Los Angeles" (pp. 274-280), "Social Activities" (pp. 234-237), and "The Sphinxes of Alameda Street" (pp. 255-259). Since these sections are readily available in the *History*, they are not included here. A fifth chapter, "Farming," has also been omitted, but in a section of his *Times* anniversary account (Ch. IX) that was deleted by Spalding in his "Autobiography" appeared a succinct paragraph covering approximately the same material:

"In the fall of 1881, my health having been impaired by long days of newspaper drudgery and too close confinement, I resigned my place in the *Express* office and moved to the country to recuperate. I undertook to subdue a bit of very brushy and very rocky land at Sierra Madre, plant it to trees and vines and make a home. Pending the period when my place should become productive, it was necessary for me to get out and hustle to keep things going: so I gradually drifted back into my old calling. For several months [beginning in December 1883] I edited the *Rural Californian*, a monthly horticultural publication conducted by George Rice. Then, for nearly a year I served on the *Press and Horticulturist* of Riverside, L. M. Holt proprietor. While thus employed my treatise, 'The Orange: Its Culture in California', was published serially. This matter was subsequently assembled and published in book form by Mr. Holt."

Chapter IX

THE *TIMES*: ITS HISTORY[1]

———————————

ON DECEMBER 4, 1881, Nathan Cole, Jr., son of a wealthy St. Louis man, and Thomas Gardiner, a former editor of the Sacramento *Union*, issued the first number of the *Times*, a morning Republican journal. Cole and Gardiner made arrangements with Yarnell, Caystile & Mathes to set up and print the new paper in the long-established Mirror office. The enterprise must also have been launched on a shoestring or else the projectors' calculations failed in some way, for in about a month they were obliged to turn their paper over to the printing firm in settlement of accrued bills.[2]

Thus it came about that Jesse Yarnell, who "wouldn't be caught dead owning a newspaper," found his firm with one on hand, and it was a youngster with a healthy appetite and very little patron-

[1]For the anniversary edition of the *Times*, Dec. 4, 1921, Spalding wrote a history of the paper with special attention to his own experiences. In his "Autobiography" he wished the article to be repeated at this point and made some deletions and changes, which have here been followed.

[2]Nathan Cole, Jr. (1860-1921), was a newspaperman in St. Louis, 1878-1880, before coming to Los Angeles. After his experience with the *Times*, he stayed with newspaper work in California and Oregon for a few years, organizing the Los Angeles *Evening Telegram* in 1882. Then his interests turned to real estate and business. He built a railroad from Los Angeles to Pasadena, developed some land in the Antelope Valley, and helped manage the San Joaquin Valley Sugar Company. Early in the twentieth century he served two terms as city police commissioner.

Thomas Gardiner retired from the *Times* after the first issue, leaving Cole to struggle along for the rest of the month. In his *History*, I, 245-246, Spalding erroneously called him James Gardiner.

age. The printing-house made the best of a bad situation by carrying the paper along. Yarnell was rather against it, but Mathes insisted that the firm could make good in that way and, to back his opinion, assumed the newspaper editing and management.[3] Mathes was a practical printer and had been foreman on the *Herald* for some time previous to joining the Mirror establishment. How much experience he had had in editorial work I do not know, but he was a man of education and lots of common sense and he put up a very good front with his new duties.

In July, 1882, Col. Harrison Gray Otis came down from Santa Barbara looking for an opening in the Los Angeles field. In the new and arduous work of carrying the paper along for six months Mr. Mathes's health had given way. When Col. Otis interviewed him on the subject of taking hold, his proposition was welcomed. The other members of the firm objected to taking in another partner, but Mathes told them that they must either do so or one of them must assume the responsibilities of running the paper; otherwise it would be discontinued, for he was physically at the end of his string. Under this powerful suasion the firm finally consented and on August 1, 1882, its title was announced as Yarnell, Caystile, Mathes & Otis, with Col. Otis as editor and manager of the *Times*.[4]

In this recital I purposely refer to our editor and manager as Colonel because that was the title he had received in the Civil War and by which we designated him at the time of these events. It would be an anachronism here to call him by the title which he received in the Philippine War, long afterwards.

Col. Otis had published the Santa Barbara *Press* for a number of years previously, and had made a spicy little paper, but he probably concluded that no great success was to be achieved in that limited field and as soon as opportunity offered he sold the property. Hence the prospecting expedition to Los Angeles for a change of base. Finding the *Times* suspended between heaven and earth, like Mohammed's coffin, he promptly decided that that was the very opening he was after.[5]

[3]Samuel Jay Mathes, born in Tennessee, came to Los Angeles in 1875. He abandoned the printing trade in the 1880's, conducted Pullman excursions, and toured the country with an exhibit about California. Newmark, p. 482; *Great Register of Los Angeles County*, 1879.

[4]The following paragraph has been moved from its original position four paragraphs later.

[5]The life of Harrison Gray Otis (1837-1917) was dominated by two themes: journalism and the Republican Party. In his native Ohio he was a printer's apprentice by the age of 14, and as a young man he became associated with the Republican Party

Some time previously A. W. Francisco, a veteran newspaper man from Cincinnati and Toledo, Ohio, had acquired some interest in the Mirror establishment, but he was a silent partner. Being from the same state as Col. Otis, and the two having worked in the same field and being friends of long standing, it is probable that he had a good deal to do with effecting the new combination.[6]

When Col. Otis bought his interest in the firm the agreed price was $5,000, of which he paid $1,000 in cash and gave his obligation for the balance. The actual money in the transaction probably represented something near the net proceeds of the Santa Barbara paper, and perhaps was nearly the sum total of his worldly goods.

Thus matters went along with the firm of Yarnell, Caystile, Mathes & Otis from Aug. 1, 1882, to October, 1883, Col. Otis managing and editing the *Times* and the *Mirror* (the latter greatly enlarged, becoming the weekly edition of the *Times*) and Mr. Mathes assisting him in the business management. In the meantime, Tom Caystile, second member of the firm, died. So the management of the job printing business was left pretty much to Jesse Yarnell. Jesse frankly acknowledged that he didn't like the work, and this extra demand must have galled him considerably. Perhaps he was restive, also, with a newspaper of more or less precarious outcome on his hands.

In the latter part of 1883, Col. H[enry] H. Boyce, a recent arrival from the East, made his appearance. He effected an agreement with Col. Otis that the two should purchase the interests of the other partners and own the establishment in equal shares between them. Accordingly, Col. Otis bought the Yarnell and Francisco holdings and Col. Boyce that of Mr. Mathes. As to the Caystile interest, I think it was in probate and had to remain in

---

not long after its formation. He served as a delegate to the Republican National Convention in 1860. After the Civil War, in which he was brevetted lieutenant colonel, he published a small local paper in Marietta, Ohio, then spent a year as foreman of the Government Printing Office in Washington. He moved to California in 1876 and thereafter, as Spalding says, edited the Santa Barbara *Press* for four years, spent two years in Alaska (which Spalding does not mention), and in 1882 came to Los Angeles and purchased an interest in the *Times*. For thirty years he was the president and active manager of the company. For his service in the Philippines during the Spanish-American War he was brevetted major general. He remained an uncompromising Republican and a strong opponent of the Progressive Movement to the end. *Dictionary of American Biography*.

[6]Andrew W. Francisco is listed in the Los Angeles directories from the mid-1880's to early 1890's variously as journalist or real-estate agent and with such firms as Byram and Co. or Francisco, Stuart and Okey.

statu quo for the time. Shortly after the new deal the Times-Mirror Company was incorporated, with a capital of $60,000 in sixty shares.

The *Times* was a bright, attractive, newsy little sheet from the beginning—with telegraphic news and a column of editorial briefs on the first page; leading editorials on the second; markets and commercial matter on the third; and local news on the fourth. From the time that Col. Otis took charge it showed marked and constant improvement, with positive opinions on all current topics and up-to-date enterprise in every feature. His tremendous personality was woven into its very fiber during its formative years.

In May, 1885, I received an invitation to join the staff of the *Times*. I was assigned to the post of telegraph editor and general assistant. In those days (before the typewriter had made its appearance[7]) the telegraph budget came on sheets of "flimsy," a thin, tough tissue paper, so that it could be easily manifolded for the several copies required. It was written in a scrawly, hurried script, prone to be blind in places, especially as the little words, such as prepositions and conjunctions, were omitted for economy in transmission. It was the task of the telegraph editor to read this carefully, supply the missing words, make the copy reasonably plain for the printer, and see that every sentence had its verb; in short, that it "made sense." Besides this, I was required to write the heads and subheads, and keep notes of the more interesting items so that I could prepare the column of editorial briefs to appear on the first page. I read proof on all telegraphic matter, and finally "put the paper to bed"—i.e., after the matter had been corrected, I stood beside the foreman at the make-up stone, and gave such suggestions as might be serviceable for its arrangement and adjustment in the last two forms. The modern metropolitan journal has quite a large contingent to perform these various functions, but I was "the cook and the captain's mate and the crew of the Nancy brig."[8] Between times I was drafted to hold copy for the Colonel, as he read proof on legal advertisements, commercial matter and all that required especial care.

[7]The typewriter, invented as early as 1829, was playing a fairly large part in the business world by the 1880's. Jackson A. Graves, a lawyer, claimed that he operated the first typewriter in Los Angeles not long after 1875. Spalding, *History*, I, 218.

[8]W. S. Gilbert, "The Yarn of the 'Nancy Bell,' " from *The "Bab" Ballads:*
"Oh, I am a cook and a captain bold,
And the mate of the *Nancy* brig,
And a bo'sun tight, and a midshipmite,
And the crew of the captain's gig."

Col. Otis wrote the political or "leading" editorials, supplied the reprint matter, read proof for the entire paper, except that portion delegated to me, and supervised everything. And you may be sure nothing was too trivial to escape his attention.

Charlie Lummis was the city editor and the entire staff for local news.[9] I think he read his own proof, but it was passed to the Colonel for a final look-over. A more indefatigable or more conscientious worker in a newspaper office I never knew than Charlie Lummis. Every day he was at his desk an hour or two ahead of the required time and, before commencing his rounds, occupied himself in pasting in a big scrapbook and indexing every item of local news that had appeared in the paper that morning. This special work was entirely on his own motion and I used to regard it as an unnecessary labor of love, but must acknowledge that in looking up past events and getting the correct history of things that are ordinarily lost in the shuffle he had the bulge on any other newsgatherer I had ever seen.

But everybody who had anything to do with the *Times* in those days worked hard and conscientiously and I have reason to believe the tradition has been handed down in the staff ever since. It was the example set by our chief more than anything else that held us so strictly in line. Exacting he was in every detail, but not more so with others than he was with himself, and, though positive, he was never harsh with his subordinates. When it came to standing between a member of his newspaper family and the outside world he was loyalty itself and a veritable stone wall. That is why the employees liked him so well and remained with him so long.

I remember a little incident of his enforcing discipline that made a deep impression and is worth recounting. Jan. 19, 1886, occurred the great overflow of the Los Angeles River, which catastrophe has come down in history. On the defile below the Arroyo Seco the river over-ran its banks, carrying away the depot building of the Los Angeles and Independence Railway. This was swept downstream, wrecking the Downey Avenue bridge just below it and every other bridge in the city. In the lower lands

[9]"Charles F. Lummis, a newspaper man of Ohio, completed his 'hike' of 3,507 miles, from Chillicothe to Los Angeles, in 143 days, and joined the staff of the *Times* [1884]. Mr. Lummis had written a series of letters during his journey, which had been published in the *Times*, and he was already well known here on his arrival. He was adopted as a favorite son at the start, and continued to be a prominent character until his death." Spalding, *History*, I, 253-254. See also Edwin R. Bingham, *Charles F. Lummis: Editor of the Southwest* (San Marino, Calif., 1955).

opposite Boyle Heights, where the Arcade Depot now stands, and between there and the river bank it spread out in a great flood, carrying away small houses and marooning many families so that they had to be helped away. It was in this work that Martin Aguirre distinguished himself, riding into the water on horseback and rescuing many people. In fact, Martin was the hero of the day and so appreciative were the people of his services that they afterward made him Sheriff of the county.[10]

Getting back to our newspaper office, Charlie Lummis, it seems, had just been guilty of some infraction of discipline (Charlie was a little hard in the mouth sometimes, as well as other people), and what did the Colonel do but assign him to the routine of reporting Council proceedings! To me he gave the work of reporting the flood.

This must have been heartbreaking business for Charlie, and it fairly took my breath away with the suddenness and magnitude of the task. But I understood military discipline well enough not to falter. Mr. Peabody was requisitioned from the business office to help me, and forth we sallied. Our report filled nearly a page of the paper, and was gotten up with all the typographical spread we knew about at that time. It would look inexpressibly tame nowadays—a single column head, not more than six inches long; but we gave it a double-leaded introduction, summarizing the mischief done; divided the field into various parts, with a section head for each, and subheads all through, winding up with a review of previous floods.

I know that Peabody and I thought it was a dandy; but all the time I had sore misgivings about Charlie Lummis. I pictured him droning away his time with that stupid Council, and fairly gnashing his teeth. And I was afraid he might feel resentment toward me, and that our hitherto pleasant relations might be broken. But Charlie was man enough to take his medicine and make no wry faces. He squared himself with the commander by doing so and the next day went back to his regular detail, as I returned to mine. We tacitly decided to call it a closed incident, and he and I never even attempted to make explanations to each other. Our mutual relations flowed along as pleasantly as ever.

About three months after the flood (March 1886) differences between Col. Otis and Col. Boyce became so acute that they de-

<hr>

[10]Spalding wrote an account of the flood in his *History*, I, 263, in which a few additional details are included, such as Harry Chandler delivering the papers to Boyle Heights in a boat and rescuing a family from a flooded house on the return.

cided to sever their business relations.[11] As usual, when two partners agree to disagree, it became a matter of "give or take." I think it was Boyce who named a figure that he was willing to pay for Otis's half-interest in the property; or he would take the same amount for his interest.

He knew that Col. Otis had very little cash in hand, and was already in debt for his holding, whereas he had quite a wad of capital, and he expected to buy at his own terms. But he underestimated the nerve of his partner. When the stock had been placed in escrow, under written agreement, Col. Otis served notice that he would buy. The price for a half-interest was fixed at $27,000, I think.

How Col. Otis managed it I never knew, as he kept his own counsel in business matters, but I have a pretty definite idea that a certain wise and long-headed banker stood by him very handsomely in his pinch, for the money had to be forthcoming at once.[12]

It was at this stage that Mr. Albert McFarland and I came into the business.[13] Mr. McFarland took a quarter interest, for which he either paid cash or arranged to carry it on his own responsibility. I had no money in hand, but expected to receive several thousand dollars shortly from the sale, already effected, of some real estate in Kansas City. So I was carried along in the general combination until I could fill on the deal. As between myself and Col. Otis or anybody else, there was not the scratch of a pen to show that I had purchased stock or could claim any interest whatever.

The following notice, which might appropriately have been headed "General Orders No. 1," was published at the head of the editorial column:

[11]By 1885 Henry Boyce's ineptness as business manager had brought the paper close to insolvency; hence the considerable ill will that developed between Boyce and Otis before Boyce was forced out in 1886.

[12]This was probably Isaias W. Hellman, judging from a comment in the Farmers and Merchants National Bank of Los Angeles, *Fifty Years of Banking Service* (Los Angeles, [1921]), p. 30: "General Harrison Gray Otis, during his lifetime, many times publicly stated that in a critical period of his career, this bank [i.e., the Farmers and Merchants Bank] loaned him money which enabled him to become the sole proprietor of the Times."

[13]Albert McFarland became the vice-president and treasurer of the corporation. Spalding considered him a close friend, affectionately calling him "Daddy" or "Father" and on occasion lending him money.

Business Announcements.

OFFICE OF

THE TIMES-MIRROR COMPANY,

Los Angeles, April 5, 1886.

The following changes in the ownership and *personnel* of THE TIMES-MIRROR COMPANY are hereby announced:

I. Harrison G. Otis has this day purchased of H. H. Boyce his entire interest in the establishment, and Mr. Boyce retires from the business.

II. Mr. Albert McFarland, a veteran journalist, of ability and experience, and with a long, honorable and successful career in the profession, has purchased an interest in the establishment, and will henceforth be actively connected with the publication of the DAILY TIMES and the WEEKLY MIRROR.

III. Mr. William A. Spalding, for many years past prominently identified with journalism in Los Angeles, and who has during the past year been a trusted and efficient member of the TIMES staff, has also purchased an interest in the establishment, and will continue his active connection with the business.

IV. Col. H. G. Otis, who has been at the editorial head of the TIMES since the first year of its existence, will continue in that capacity, and will have, besides, the general direction of the Company's affairs. The policy of the paper will continue unchanged. That policy is, in brief, the maintenance of the principles of the Republican party, the defense of liberty, law and public morals, and the up-building of the city and county of Los Angeles and the State of South California. The motto of the now united proprietors will be, "PUSH THINGS!"

At a little later date I made good on my obligation, and received my stock. Later still, Mr. Rhodes purchased five shares in behalf of his daughter, Mrs. Dorothea Lummis, who was on the staff.[14] The new order of things worked smoothly within the establishment from the beginning.

Perhaps a few words as to the plant of the Times-Mirror Company at that time might be interesting. We occupied for our business office a room about twenty by thirty feet in area on the ground-floor of Downey Block, corner of Temple and New High streets.

Beneath this had been excavated a cellar—it would not be proper to call it a basement, for the light of day scarcely reached it and the ceiling was very low. It had probably been put in as a makeshift to accommodate the heavy press when the Mirror es-

[14]Dorothea Rhodes and Charles Lummis were married while Dorothea was a medical student at Boston University and Charles a junior at Harvard. The two were divorced in 1890. She became president of the Los Angeles County Homeopathic Medical Society and a leader in the societies for the Prevention of Cruelty to Animals and Prevention of Cruelty to Children. Later she married Ernest Carroll Moore.

tablishment first undertook the printing of the *Times* for Gardiner & Cole. The press, one of the Taylor or Potter stop-cylinder type, was operated by a water motor not bigger than a bushel basket. Linc Crawford was the pressman.

He told me about a serious difficulty which he once encountered when a small fish came down in the supply pipe and clogged the motor. The publication of the paper was delayed until the supply could be shut off, the motor taken apart and the fish extracted. It was a sort of fishing that was no sport for Linc.

On the second floor, from a point about midway of the block facing Temple Street to the New High Street side, were the editorial-room, the composing-room and the job-printing plant. The editorial-room was about 20 x 20 feet, and was reached by a flight of steps midway of the block on Temple Street, or probably adjacent to the business office. From the head of the stairs on the left, and extending to the New High Street end of the building, came the composing-room of the paper and the job-printing plant. The job presses were operated by foot power. From the composing-room to the pressroom below a chute or "dumb waiter" ran through one side of the business office, which contrivance served to lower and raise the forms.

And this suggests another one of our early mishaps. About 1 or 2 o'clock one morning the aforesaid dumb waiter went wrong, tumbling a form to the basement and making hopeless "pi" of the whole thing. This was a serious calamity for a concern having no greater mechanical facilities than ours, and the foreman, Frank Eddy, sent post-haste for Father McFarland, the manager, to see if he could suggest any way out of the dilemma. When Mr. McFarland had taken in the situation, he said: "I tell you what we can do, boys. There is a real estate map in the job office, made just to the size of a page. We'll get that and run it as an advertisement, and nobody will know that anything has happened."

"But, Mr. McFarland," said the foreman, "that would be against the rules of the union—unless you agree to pay to the chapel the full price of setting the page in the smallest type (nonpareil) used in the paper."[15]

15The chapel was a shop subdivision of the printers' union. Spalding in "How the Trouble Commenced" (pp. 3-4 of MS in possession of Mrs. Helen Groff) described the *Times* chapel in detail as "a more or less democratic body comprising all of the printers who held regular cases. This Chapel might be called into session around a composing stone at any time before or after working hours to discuss and settle by majority vote matters of minor detail between the printers themselves or between them and the foreman. Sometimes they made a decision by 'jeffing.' That is, one of the printers delegated thereto held in his closed hand a number of types which he threw

I suppose the difficulty was met in that way, but it went against the grain with all of us. We had already paid for preparing the page in the job office, but by an arbitrary rule established by the union, unknown to us, we were prevented from using our own property to help ourselves out of a bad predicament, unless we paid an exorbitant bonus to the compositors for work they had not performed. I cite this instance to show the mean and tyrannous exactions to which we were subjected when the composing-room was under union domination.

Boyce had gone out with a grouch against Col. Otis and the whole *Times* outfit. With a comfortable sum of cash at his disposal, he sailed high for a time, appearing first as president of a new bank, established by L. N. Breed and associates, located in the Nadeau Block, corner of Spring and First streets. But he continued in that position only a few months.[16] Not long afterward Boyce, with Harry Payne and several other associates, launched a new morning Republican paper—the *Tribune*. It should be called *Tribune* No. 1, to distinguish it from the paper bearing the same name projected in comparatively recent times by E. T. Earl. Let the reader bear in mind that there was no connection between the two enterprises. From the passing of No. 1 to the advent of No. 2 there was a long interval.[17]

---

upon the composing stone. The issue was determined by the number of 'nicks' that were on top when the types were at rest. It was very similar to casting dice, and a mere matter of chance. The Chapel also discharged a business function, receiving and disbursing patronage and money. The Nonpareil cases were regarded as especially desirable because in this finest type a competent printer could set more thousands in a given time than in the coarser Brevier or Bourgeois that made up the body of the paper. The market and stock reports and the commercial matter generally were set in Nonpareil. Some of this was in tabular form, involving considerable 'pick-ups' from forms already standing, and some of it was paid price and a half. These were called 'fat takes', and the Nonpareil holdings were 'fat cases'. It was the custom in Chapel to dispose of the 'fat cases' by auction, the printer bidding the highest premium in thousands of M's to take them. Out of his earnings on the 'fat case' the holder was required to pay the proceeds of his premium to the head of the Chapel, and by him it was disbursed in equal shares to the other members. There was other 'fat' that found its way into Chapel hands, such as half pay assessed against the office for cuts introduced into reading matter, where in most cases no matter had been set. It was grossly unjust, as against the office; but no matter, it was one of the rules of the Union, and the Chapel divided the loot."

[16]The Southern California National Bank was organized in May 1886. Boyce was succeeded by John J. Redick as president. Levi Newton Breed was vice-president from the beginning, becoming president a few years later.

[17]"October 4th [1886] appeared the first issue of the *Los Angeles Tribune*, edited and managed by Col. H. H. Boyce. The paper was of good size, well printed and newsy, so far as local affairs were concerned . . . . The new paper smashed precedents in the old town by issuing every morning in the year. . . . When the *Tribune* broke

Boyce's *Tribune* set out with a considerable flourish, for there was plenty of money behind it, and justice compels me to say that it was an attractive paper in many ways. Prof. Charles Frederick Holder and Col. F. A. Eastman, the latter a newspaper man of Chicago, held the editorial chair successively, and good talent was employed to gather the local news.[18] But the paper lacked moral backbone, and betrayed too obviously that the one object of its existence was to get a knife into the *Times*. It had no Associated Press franchise, and for outside news depended upon a few special dispatches, what it could fake in the office, and what it could steal from us.

Well, the *Tribune* fought its dubious way for several years, until it had sunk all of Boyce's money and all the money he could induce his friends to put into the enterprise, and then it turned up its toes. A month or two afterward, its effects were sold at auction. Col. Otis attended the sale, I remember, and bought a few little tricks, not that he needed them exactly, but just for souvenirs.

As the *Times* had grown steadily from the time of its reorganization, notwithstanding the opposition, we began to be very cramped in our quarters and with our limited mechanical facilities. So we looked for something better. About that time Dan McFarland (son of our associate) bought from Frank Carpenter a tract of four lots running through from Spring to Fort Street (now Broadway) taking in all the intervening First Street frontage. He was about to subdivide this and sell it by the front foot, and in order to impart some momentum to the sale, as well as for personal reasons, he offered us extra inducements to take the corner on First and Fort. We bought it, and with a moderate

---

over the line, the other morning papers were obliged to do the same." Spalding, *History*, I, 263. *Tribune* No. 1 ceased on Dec. 5, 1890.

The second *Tribune* ran from July 4, 1911, to July 4, 1918, under editorship of Edwin T. Earl, developer of refrigerated railroad cars for fresh fruit and also owner of the *Express* from 1901 till his death in 1919.

[18]Charles Frederick Holder, a Massachusettsan educated at the Friends' School in Providence and the U. S. Naval Academy, worked in the New York Museum of Natural History, 1870-1876. For his health he moved to Pasadena in 1885. He wrote voluminously on natural history and about southern California and was elected to the chair of zoology at the Throop Institute (later California Institute of Technology). Stimson (*Labor Movement*, p. 105) lists J. H. Morrow as an associate with Holder on the *Tribune* in 1890. Holder later worked for the San Francisco *Examiner*. John P. Young, *Journalism in California* (San Francisco, [1915]), p. 160.

Francis A. Eastman appears in the city directories of 1887 and 1888 as editor of the *Tribune*, but he is not listed as such in 1890.

cash payment, a transfer of some *Times* stock, and securing the balance by mortgage on a piece of real estate owned by myself (corner of Fort and Temple streets), we got title to the new lot free. Then we secured a loan nearly sufficient to erect the building, depending on our earnings to defray a small part of the outlay. Thus did we exemplify Col. Otis's motto, "Push things." And, considering the original thousand dollars with which he had begun operations a few years before; the fact that he had bought out his disgruntled partner for $27,000, cash down, and had taken in new partners with comparatively little money; that we were now launching out to put up a building of our own at an expense of about $50,000, perhaps it may be fairly stated that we were going—some.

And that was far from being the end of the story. We had to acquire new and improved printing machinery, more type, more of everything, fit up a new office and move. A Hoe perfecting press and a steam engine to drive it were installed in the basement of the new building. Think what a jump from our Taylor cylinder and its water motor! And all this was done in the face of a daily battle waged by Mr. Boyce's jealous *Tribune*.

But I am getting somewhat ahead of my story. While we were still in the old quarters the Mirror job office secured the contract for printing the *Great Register* of the county. This was the biggest thing going in the printing line at that time. The *Great Register* contained the name, address, age, etc., of every voter in the county, and a considerable edition had to be published. It was going to tax the facilities of our job office to the utmost to accomplish the work in time for the next election.

On the newspaper side we had Mr. Boyce's *Tribune* in the full flush of its starting and to meet his bluff we had been compelled to issue seven papers a week. That meant that the staff had to work seven days instead of six, as formerly. At this juncture [September 1886] Col. Otis was waited upon one Saturday afternoon about 5 o'clock by a committee of strangers, who informed him that they represented the Typographical Union. They brought him as an ultimatum the message that our job office must be "squared" within an hour or the printers would not go to work at 6 o'clock to set up the Sunday paper.

Short shrift, that, and no courtesies wasted! With equal grace they might have presented revolvers and told us to throw up our hands. The Mirror printing concern had been run for years as an "open office." That is, it had made no distinction in employment, some of the men belonging to the union, some not. The newspaper office of the *Times*, however, was entirely under the domination of the union and it was by special stipulation with that organization that the job office had been left "open." To square it now meant that every nonunion employee in that department must be discharged without an hour's notice.

Col. Otis's military instinct was quick enough to show him that he was surrounded and that there was nothing for him to do but surrender; however, he would not do so without a parley. And what do you think he parleyed about and insisted on and would not give in until it was stipulated? Why, that those nonunion men in the job office should not be thus summarily thrown out. There was that loyalty to his staff that I mentioned some way back. The final arrangement was that those faithful, long-time employees should be given the privilege of joining the union and keeping their jobs. So the impending destruction was averted, but you may rest assured that this episode rankled in the hearts of all of us.[19]

From this time forth the demands of the union became more exacting and oppressive. I will not attempt to catalog the grievances we had, but let it suffice that finally a regulation was adopted, without consulting us, taking away our right to hire or discharge the printers in our composing-room—that function was relegated to the foreman. We finally decided that if we expected to control own our business we must break away from such dictation and thralldom.

One day while we were discussing the situation, I told Col. Otis about a printers' organization in Kansas City that worked on a different plan. It was known as the Printers' Protective Fraternity, and it had held its ground in the *Journal* office for a number of years. That organization believed in fair dealing with employers, and if it had any complaint to make, acted on its own

[19]The printers were the pioneers of Los Angeles organized labor, having started the Typographical Union in 1875. The *Star* had agreed to give preference to union printers in 1878. In 1882 a minor dispute in the *Times* between union compositors and nonunion job printers was satisfactorily settled. During this early period when Otis was still new on the paper, the *Times* was friendly to organized labor. The dismissal in 1883 of an assistant foreman, allegedly because of union affiliation, brought on a strike. Neither Otis nor the union, however, was sufficiently strong to force the other's hand, and, because Otis needed labor, by 1884, as Spalding says, the *Times* was completely staffed by union members. In 1885 the *Times* had remained friendly to the union during a strike of the rival *Express*. In 1886 Otis' capitulation to the demands for unionization of the Times-Mirror job office was, as Spalding implies, dictated by the need to fulfill the contract for the *Great Register*, but, as Stimson suggests (*Labor Movement*, p. 73), Boyce's *Tribune*, beginning on October 4 its anti-*Times*, prounion appeal, may also have influenced the decision.

initiative, without outside dictation and settled its own affairs.[20] Years before, I had been an employee of the *Journal*, and thus knew about the matter. Col. Otis requested me to take the subject up and get fuller information, so I wrote to Mr. J. A. Mann, the manager, stating our situation and requirements.

The upshot of the correspondence was that we engaged a force of some twenty men—all members of the Printers' Protective Fraternity—to come to Los Angeles and take charge of our newspaper and job offices. By the time this was brought about we had moved into our new building. When the force of Kansas City printers arrived, I met them at the depot and escorted them to the *Times* office.

Arrangements had already been made for the lodging and board of the new force, so no time had to be wasted in preliminaries, and that very day we informed the union men that we would dispense with their services.[21] Our flank movement had taken them entirely by surprise. They called it a "lock-out" and appealed to the public for sympathy on that score, but what had they done to us in the matter of giving notice, when they had us in a corner?

Then, of course, the big fight was on.[22] The disgruntled printers boycotted our paper, terrorized our patrons until the advertising business of the merchants was nearly all withdrawn, and

[20]The Printers' Protective Fraternity, organized on a national scale in Kansas City in 1886, was a rival of the International Typographical Union, the local of which had been dealing with the *Times*. Fraternity members had been imported into San Diego in 1887 during a labor conflict, and the fear of such importation was constant with the I.T.U. The Fraternity opposed strikes as well as lockouts and admitted proprietors and stockholders to membership. Because of Otis' support, Los Angeles became its national headquarters after the turn of the century.

[21]Pauline Jacobson, after an interview many years later with a man who had been on the scene, described the event rather more dramatically: "Otis appeared in the composing-room. Rage was swelling his neck and purpling his face and the veins in his forehead as he raised one fist, bringing it down with full force, shouting: " 'Every — — man get out of here! And get out — — quick!' " Quoted in Stimson, *Labor Movement*, p. 106.

[22]The strike of the Typographical Union began in August 1890, against all four daily papers in the city, but soon centered on the *Times*. Earlier that year management had asked the unions for pay reductions on the grounds that the printers were still getting boom wages after the boom had collapsed. In spite of depressed labor conditions, the unions refused. After the strike was under way and the union had made some concessions, the *Express* and the *Tribune* capitulated on August 8. The *Herald* stood with the *Times* until Ayers gave in on October 12. Thereafter the union settled in for a long boycott of the *Times* lasting until April 7, 1892, when the union accepted some minor concessions from Otis.

One of the interesting points in Spalding's account is the apparent fact, which the union movement long suspected, that Otis had arranged with the Printers' Protective Fraternity before the strike began.

they even bulldozed the boys so that it was dangerous to try to sell the *Times* on the street. The unions of San Francisco sent down their craftiest and most determined strike organizers and a fund of $10,000 for their use.[23]

But the waves of discord rolled against the stone castle on the corner in vain and broke of their own momentum. We did not bother to meet their attacks or answer their charges, contenting ourselves with a plain statement of the case to the public, and then we bided our time—and sawed wood. We got out the newsiest paper we could every day, filling the space vacated by some of the timid merchants with good reading matter. After a month or two of this sort of fighting, the merchants, seeing that nothing serious was likely to happen, began to get their courage, and when Father Mac and I dropped in on them and showed that we were not excited or scared and talked the matter over in a sensible way, they began to come back into our columns. Once well started, they all came with a run.

It was a question of the *Times* showing some nerve; that was all. The net result of the first year's agitation was that the unions had blown in $10,000 and the *Times* had made just about that sum, net profit. And this profit came very handy to help pay for our new building.

Looking back at those strenuous days shortly after our change of location, I remember Harry Chandler as a rather burly country lad who was part owner, with a man named Richardson, in the *Times* routes. He joined the force in 1885. He had a great fund of good humor, was full of pep, and wide awake to everything that was going on. It did not take long to find that he was of bigger caliber than the average circulator, and gradually things drifted into his hands until one fine day he was installed as superintendent of city circulation. But everybody knows the rest of that story.[24]

Mrs. Eliza A. Otis was a reliable and a devoted worker. Her departments, "The Saunterer" and "Susan Sunshine," were always supplied on time and in full measure, and besides these she frequently contributed poems of merit. Her "Susan Sunshine"

[23]The union received $8,032 in the year before May 1891. Of that, $3,091 came from outside unions, including $2,600 from the San Francisco Typographical Union. The remainder of the $8,032 came from assessments and dues of local members. Stimson, *Labor Movement*, p. 112.

[24]Harry Chandler began his career as a clerk in the circulation department of the *Times*, advanced to manager of that department, and in 1917 became president of the corporation and publisher of the *Times*.

columns discussed matters of special interest to women, and "The Saunterer" dealt with the philosophy of life, morals and religion, free from dogmatism or stilted preaching. Her writings all appealed to the better impulses and the kindlier moods of her readers, and without doubt contributed as much as any single influence to the moral standing of the paper, making it a welcome visitor in the best homes.[25]

Miss Marian Otis (now Mrs. Harry Chandler) was a member of the business staff for a number of years after we became established in our building. She was of a quiet, forceful, self-contained temperament, very efficient and reliable, pleasant in her dealings with everybody, and she gained the esteem of her associates and the good-will of patrons.[26]

Frank Pfaffinger was bookkeeper for the drygoods establishment of G. Y. Smith & Co., Kansas City, when in 1887 the *Times* invited him to come to Los Angeles, take charge of its books, and see if he could fill the bill. He did.[27]

Harry Brook joined the staff in 1886. But in those days we did not call him "Doctor," just Harry.[28]

Of the very early personnel, I know of none except the three above named who still remain. George W. Burton, who went over to the Great Majority only a short time ago, came in at a later date than I have been writing about.[29]

Much might be said concerning the successive improvements

[25]Eliza A. Wetherby married H. G. Otis in 1859. She was an active journalist till her death in 1904.

[26]Marian Otis, second daughter of H. G. Otis, married Harry Chandler on June 5, 1894, while he was circulation manager of the *Times*.

[27]Frank X. Pfaffinger was a Bavarian cabinetmaker who came to America in 1882 and attended Spalding's Commercial College in Kansas City. It was probably through William Spalding's brother that the *Times* heard of him. Pfaffinger arrived in Los Angeles "at 3:00 o'clock a.m., March 27, 1887, and reported to the Times office at 6:00 o'clock in the morning.

"There was no one to report to, but the two-revolution cylinder press was still going in the press room, and as they were short of hands, he helped fold papers. At that time it was a four-page sheet, and had to be folded by hand.

"Mr. Pfaffinger is now [1931] treasurer of the Times-Mirror Company." Spalding, *History*, III, 627.

[28]Harry Ellington Brook began working for the *Times* soon after his arrival in Los Angeles. He was employed as an editorial writer and also wrote pamphlets for the Chamber of Commerce. In June 1894 with Frank A. Pattee and Charles D. Willard he started the *Land of Sunshine*, which was shortly thereafter taken over by Charles Lummis.

[29]George W. Burton founded one of the early private schools in Los Angeles (the Burton School, later known as the College of Los Angeles). After his school closed, Burton went to Oregon; then returned to become an editorial writer and railroad and market reporter on the *Times*. He died Oct. 28, 1921.

in the mechanical plant, for the concern went forward with leaps and bounds after we became well settled in our own building, had assisted in the obsequies of the *Tribune*, and had drawn the teeth of the strikers. When we put in the Mergenthaler linotype machines, being one of the first half dozen newspapers in the United States—in the world, for that matter—to do so, it was a great advance. When we added our second Hoe perfecting press, it was another. And then, in a few years came the third. One of the strong peculiarities of the *Times* was that it always kept so far in advance of its competitors in mechanical equipment. Sometimes when we were facing a new outlay of $40,000 or $50,000 for such purpose, some of us were apt to question whether the Colonel's forward vision might not be oversanguine, but events always proved that he had not unduly anticipated the growth of the community or the advance of the business.[30]

I have said nothing about the many campaigns made by the *Times* in the old days on political and local issues, and just to touch upon them briefly would require a paper longer than this. In a word, it might be said that the *Times* never took an equivocal or a wobbly attitude on any question—it was always positive and outspoken one way or the other. And when it announced a position, it always stood by it to the end. It was in favor of clean politics, and against cliques and rings seeking to subserve selfish ends in any party. It opposed the Southern Pacific machine as long as that combination sought to dominate the politics of the State. It championed the free harbor cause, against C. P. Huntington and all his cohorts, and was a mighty factor in achieving that victory, justly meriting the memorial tablet that was set by grateful citizens in the wall of its first building, and which was rescued unharmed, and still bears testimony in the present structure.[31] It has upheld the American principle of free labor, and it has accomplished more in the way of making Los Angeles industrially independent and correspondingly prosperous today than any other influence.

---

[30]A paragraph has here been deleted, the content of which is found in Ch. X.

[31]"This tablet placed here by the people of Los Angeles commemorates their appreciation of the effective services of the Los Angeles Times in the contest for a free harbor at San Pedro, April 27, 1899."

Chapter X

A NEWSPAPERMAN

IN REAL ESTATE (1885-1893)

WHEN I BEGAN WORK on the *Times*, in May, 1885, I lodged with a Spanish family on Buena Vista Street, near the office. Later I took lodging at the home of Dr. Pigné-Dupuytren, on Temple Street, near Grand Avenue.[1] As we published no paper on Monday, that left me free to visit the family at Sierra Madre on Sunday. My faithful Chinaman, Ahn Goon, took care of the farm work, and Mary had her father and mother a part of the time, and Aunt Ann another part, and either Mrs. Poultney or Mrs. Gaskell to cook and help with the children.[2]

Every ounce of my energy was taken by the paper, and my weekly visit did not enable me to be a factor in the management of the household. All I could do was to pay the bills. My newspaper work was practically all at night, beginning about five or six o'clock in the afternoon, and continuing until three in the morning.

Philip J. Marley was a *rara avis* among newspaper men. He

[1]Dr. J. B. Pigné-Dupuytren (1807-1886) was a physician with degrees from Heidelberg and Edinburgh, who came to the California gold fields in 1849 and was thereafter active in French affairs in San Francisco. He moved to Los Angeles in 1875, tried his hand at the French paper *L'Union*, then helped found *Le Progrès* in 1884, subsequently serving as its editor for one year. He was involved in the city's real-estate and educational life, as he was in the practice of medicine. Fred Wood married his daughter, Leona. Bissell, "French Language Press," pp. 330-331.

[2]Ahn Goon was with the family only during the Sierra Madre years. Some of Spalding's poems ("Too Hay" and "Ah Get and You Bet") involve humorous characters with similar names (Ah Goo and N' Goon); but Mrs. Helen Groff, knowing her father's great respect for Ahn Goon, does not feel Spalding would have used him as a model for such jokes.

A section has here been omitted in which Spalding describes the birth of Helen Spalding Groff, Dec. 24, 1885, and her early illnesses.

was foreman on the *Express* for ten or twelve years, and a more steady and reliable foreman never made up forms. If he had any bad habits, I never discovered what they were. I never heard him utter an angry or a profane word.[3] His wife was of Irish extraction, with brilliant social qualities, and the possessor of a fine, well-trained voice. She and Madame Marra were the favorite singers in all of our local entertainments. There were two children, a girl and a boy. But, with all his good qualities, Marley was not able to retain the love and loyalty of his brilliant wife. She eloped with Dr. Lockhart, taking her girl, about twelve years old, with herself and paramour. Dr. Lockhart deserted a wife and several children. The runaways located in Spokane, Washington. Marley retained the boy, Eddie, about eight or nine years old. So far as I know, Marley made no effort to follow the runaways or get his wife back, but in a few months he went into quick consumption, and within a year died. I interested myself in him during his sickness, and after his death, applied for letters of administration on his estate and the guardianship of his children. There being no other applicant, the court appointed me to that position. Marley left several pieces of property and a modest sum in bank. I found a good boarding place for the boy, and took over the management of the property. I made no effort to get the daughter away from her mother, however. A few weeks later, Mrs. Marley slipped down to Los Angeles and kidnaped the boy. The court made an allowance for the support of the children and this sum I sent them in Spokane. When the children came of age I turned over to them the balance of cash remaining in my hands and quite a valuable piece of property. But I never had any dealings with Mrs. Marley, who I suppose afterwards became Mrs. Lockhart.

An exciting boom in country property occurred in 1886 and 1887. Taking advantage of this, I went into the booming business myself. Percy Wilson had sold his farm, adjoining mine, to a Dr. Pinney. I made arrangements with the doctor to join issues, and we subdivided the forty-acre piece into town lots, and placed it on the market under the title "Spalding's and Pinney's Subdivision of Lot 16, Sierra Madre Tract." We bought an entire page in a Sunday issue of the *Times* to display a plat of our tract, and the scheme was off at a gallop. We held our property interests separate, each receiving his proceeds and conveying title individually, so there was no pooling of the actual business. With-

[3]Philip J. Marley appears in the city and county directories from 1883/84 to 1886/87 as a job printer. He published the city ordinances in 1884.

out organized selling arrangements or further publicity, the lots went off very well, and in a few months I disposed of all my holdings, except an acre, reserved with the idea that I might wish to locate a country home there some day. For land which I had originally purchased at $50 an acre, I thus realized approximately $1,000 an acre. Of course the proceeds were not all cash in hand. I took notes and return mortgages for deferred payments, but these debts were eventually met. Thus the speculative element came to my rescue a second time with a great flourish to save me from a precarious investment.

I realized early that my little farm was not practical in its choice or in its planting. If I had carried it through to full fruition, it would not have produced enough, at going prices, to support my family. The ten acres of grapes would have yielded very little revenue, and the mixed orchard must have been a disappointment. The land was more valuable for town lots in an aesthetic suburban town than for any other purpose. As Sierra Madre has grown along these lines, I suppose that not one of the lots which I sold at what I considered a fancy price could be bought now for less than five to ten times what I received for it. This sale of my subdivided property placed me in possession of ready funds to an extent that I had never before experienced. I invested my money in city realty. From my cousin, Will Hurlbut, I bought a little cottage on Workman Street, East Side, for $1,200, which was afterwards sold for $1,445. I bought from George P. McLain his home place on the northeast corner of Fort and Temple streets, which was coming in for business, paying therefor $5,000.[4] I also invested in a city subdivision scheme. My friends George Safford and Henry O'Melveny and myself formed a syndicate, and purchased from Marco Forster a block of land on the East Side, fronting on Downey Avenue (now North Broadway), lying between Gates and Thomas streets.[5] We paid $20,000. This block we platted, and without any advertising or much personal effort, sold all the lots on the avenue frontage, and all but one on Gates Street. I purchased one of the avenue lots, about the middle of the block, which I thought would be serviceable for our city home. The rest of the property, extending back

[4]George P. McLain helped organize the first volunteer fire department in the early 1870's and was city engineer from 1873 to 1876. In 1887 with Martin Lehman he opened the Tivoli Opera House. He was city councilman in 1889-1890 and 1900-1902.

[5]Henry O'Melveny was a son of H. K. S. O'Melveny.

Marcos Antonio Forster's father was Don Juan Forster, the Englishman who ranched lands once owned by the Mission San Juan Capistrano. Until the early 1880's Marcos ran cattle on the Forster ranch.

on the hill, I subsequently acquired from my partners, and also bought back from Mr. Earle two lots on Gates Street, giving me three lots on that street and seven on Thomas. This is the home place which I subsequently improved, and which the family has occupied for the past thirty-two years.[6]

I served on the staff of the *Times* twelve [eight] years, and successively filled the positions of telegraph editor, city editor, manager of the Printing and Binding House, and editorial writer. Under Col. Otis's management the *Times* became a political factor, and was chiefly instrumental in securing the nomination of Col. H. H. Markham for Governor, and his election.[7] Col. Markham paid a part of his political obligation to the *Times* by appointing me to the newly instituted Building and Loan Commission. This came to me May 26th, 1897 [i.e., 1893].

I find that twenty-eight years have elapsed since my active connection with the *Times* was concluded; but during all this period I have retained a small holding of stock in the concern, and have never ceased to regard myself—even when conducting another paper—as a member of the *Times* family.[8]

[6]2434 Gates Street, Los Angeles. In 1943 the house was sold to the Carmelite Sisters who used it as a part of their Little Flower Missionary Home for girls. In 1954 the old home was demolished to make space for modern buildings.

A long section has here been omitted, which concerns Spalding's building of two houses—one on Downey Avenue and the other on Temple Street. They were financed partly through stock in the Metropolitan Building and Loan Association. The family moved to the Temple Street house from Sierra Madre in 1886 and remained till 1898 when, finding encroaching oil wells disagreeable, they lived in rented houses for a few years and then moved to their Gates Street home. In the deleted section Spalding bemoans the fact that he did not use some of his housing money to maintain his full quarter interest in the *Times*.

A group of relatives and friends, including his father and mother, came to Los Angeles about 1886, and Spalding also arranged housing for them.

[7]Henry Harrison Markham, a New Yorker and Civil War veteran, moved to Pasadena from Wisconsin in 1879. In 1884 he represented the Sixth District in Congress; he was elected governor of the state in 1890 and served for one term.

[8]This last paragraph has been taken from a deleted section of Spalding's *Times* anniversary account (Ch. IX). It replaces a short passage dealing with Spalding's first collection of verse, *My Vagabonds*, which he published privately in 1889.

In his "Autobiography" Spalding intended three chapters following this one: "Excursions in Science," "The Beginning of a Great Museum," and "Dabbling with the Occult." The second of the three can be found in the *History*, I, 366-370; the first and third have been omitted as not pertinent to the journalistic aspects of Spalding's life.

One episode of these years not mentioned in this chapter is Spalding's involvement in the organization of the local citrus industry. In 1891 he helped establish and served as vice-president of an Orange Growers' Union. On the morning of April 4, 1893, the Union dissolved, and that afternoon Spalding presided over the meetings which led to the formation of the California Fruit Growers Exchange. Spalding, "Early Chapters in History of California Citrus Culture," *California Citrograph*, VII (Jan.-March 1922), 66 *et seq.*

Chapter XI

RETURN TO THE *HERALD*

(1897-1900)

[Spalding served as California Building and Loan Commissioner (the first, along with George A. Fisher of San Francisco) at the modest salary of $200 a month from 1893 to 1897. The legislature had created the commission, as Spalding said, "to officially examine and in a way supervise the associations already extant, to check certain tendencies that had begun to crop up, and to keep out fakirs who might seek to invade the charmed circle."]

D URING MY FOUR YEARS' TERM the political complexion of the State Government changed, Governor [James H.] Budd, a Democrat, succeeding Gov. Markham. I saw there was no chance for my reappointment, and in fact was not sorry to quit, since I did not greatly enjoy the roving life that was imposed. Shortly before the close of my term I received overtures from Abbott Kinney, who had purchased from the Creightons the Los Angeles *Herald*, or at least had taken it in to keep it from bankruptcy.[1] He offered me the position of editor

---

[1]Abbott Kinney was described by Newmark (p. 519) as "a student of law and medicine, commission merchant, a botanical expert, cigarette manufacturer and member of the United States Geological Survey." He was much more, including real-estate developer (the town of Venice was one of his most ambitious ventures), country gentleman on his estate, Kinneloa, at Sierra Madre, and friendly student of the Indian. His purchase of the *Herald* was Feb. 2-3, 1897.

William S. Creighton had been editor of the *Herald*, 1895-1897, and Telfair Creighton, president of the corporation. They are not to be confused with W. W. Creighton, Spalding's earlier friend on the *Herald* and *Republican*.

and manager at the same salary I had been receiving from the State. I accepted his proposition rather gladly, as it offered a return to my profession, and a commanding position on the paper with which I had before been identified.

The *Herald* was still straight-out Democratic in politics, but it had lost prestige through a succession of bad or indifferent managements, both in its editorial columns and its business department. Mechanically it was in bad shape, the printing plant being located in a ramshackle two-story wooden building on San Pedro Street. There was a very nice, stylish office and editorial room on the ground floor of Bradbury Block on Third Street, but it was a long distance from the plant and therefore unsatisfactory. I worked under Mr. Kinney's ownership for several months, and managed things without undue friction, although I did not like him personally. It would have been to my advantage if I had liked him better and allowed him to finance the institution longer. But my friends Frank Gibson and Fred Wood came along with a scheme, backed by abundant capital, to purchase both the *Herald* and the *Express* and effect great economies by establishing them in the same printing plant, and having them co-operate in various ways. I fell for this scheme, as it would take me into the house of my friends, and seemed to show a way out from the muddle that the *Herald* was in.[2]

[2]The *Times*, Feb. 6, 1897, presented an interesting, if biased, account of developments in the *Herald*, headed "Facilis Descensus: the Pitiable Decadence of a Local Journal": "After Messrs. Ayers and Lynch sold out [October 1894], the rapid slide of the paper down the journalistic scale commenced in earnest. It was purchased by a stock corporation, composed of Los Angeles citizens, among whom were men of good intentions, but none with any practical knowledge of the newspaper business. . . . During a period of little more than one year from the time when Messrs. Ayers and Lynch sold out, the Herald was presided over successively by A. M. Stephens, Esq.; John Bradbury and William Lacy.

"A silly trick of the Herald about this time was to offer as premiums to subscribers, so-called 'town lots' of twenty-five feet front, out on an extension of the Mojave desert, in the Antelope Valley.

". . . Another change in the management was necessary. It took place in 1895, when a control in the paper was acquired by W. S. Creighton and Telfair Creighten [sic], two young persons who knew as little about the newspaper business as they do about the law. . . . Under their control, the Herald has been characterized by unadulterated faking, fraud and gross lack of ordinary business sense. . . . It was an out-and-out Popocratic journal, pandering to the baser instincts of the populace, and disgusting its old-time Democratic subscribers, who left it by scores and hundreds. . . .

"Now, under the latest change of management, there is a prospect that the Herald may do better. With Stephen M. White as one of the owners, and such men as J. W. Francis and T. E. Gibbon on the board of directors, and with a practical and experienced newspaper man like W. A. Spalding in charge, there is reasonable ground for believing that the Herald may be ultimately placed on a legitimate business basis as a prosperous newspaper enterprise."

But this requires that I should bring up some delinquent history that has been overlooked in our narrative. While I was serving on the Building and Loan Commission, important things were happening for some of my friends in Los Angeles. One was that Frank Gibson had been installed as Cashier of the First National Bank. There had been a financial flurry and a run on the bank, so that it was obliged to close its doors. Frank had taken hold in the emergency, and rendered such splendid service in working through a re-financing scheme to put the bank on its feet again, that, when the institution was reopened, he was called to the important position I have named. Fred Wood had been brought in from the San Gabriel Winery to take the position of General Manager of the electric and cable systems of street railways lately acquired by Mr. Huntington.[3] These two close friends were in commanding positions, and when they told me there was abundant capital behind their scheme to purchase the two newspapers, I knew they were sure of their ground. So I refused to close a contract with Mr. Kinney, and threw my influence in favor of the new combination. Mr. Kinney sold his stock to our people, and the *Express* was also purchased. I made my own deal for *Herald* stock, taking to the amount of $10,000, for which I gave my note to Mr. Kinney. Under the new arrangement I continued as editor and manager of the *Herald*. My friends Charlie Willard and Fred Alles were installed as editor and as manager, respectively, of the *Express*.[4] It developed later that the "abundant capital" which was available for this combination scheme was supplied by members of the City Water Company, of whom I. W. Hellman, President of the Farmers' and Merchants' Bank, was the representative and spokesman. The Water Company was then dealing with the city in the matter of surrendering its lease of the works. Under the contract, which ran fifty years, the city

[3]Henry E. Huntington, nephew and heir of Collis P. Huntington, was developer of the Pacific Electric Railway system.

[4]Charles Dwight Willard (1860-1914), graduate of the University of Michigan in 1883, by 1897 had already worked on the *Times* and the *Herald* and had helped found the *Land of Sunshine*, which later became Lummis' *Out West*.

Fred Lind Alles had worked on newspapers in Pennsylvania and Illinois before coming to California. In 1884 he purchased the *Rural Californian*, a monthly horticultural magazine which Spalding edited. It is here that the two men got to know one another. In 1887 Alles served as managing editor of the Riverside *Daily Press*, which Spalding had edited as the *Press and Horticulturist* a few years before. Returning to Los Angeles in 1889, Alles worked successively as editorial writer for the *Herald*, as business manager of the *Express*, and after 1902 as president of his own Alles Printing Company. Spalding, *History*, II, 376-377; Charles A. Moody, "Makers of Los Angeles," *Out West*, XXX (April 1909), 314.

reserved the right to reacquire the works on payment of a sum determined by arbitrators mutually appointed.[5] I suppose the stockholders of the Company (a closed corporation) thought that, during this deal, which would involve much discussion and perhaps engender partizanship and get into the hands of the politicians, it would be well to have a friendly or complaisant press on their side. Whatever they may have thought, nothing was said to me on the subject when I was put in charge of the *Herald*, and when I finally sized up the situation, I made up my mind that the *Herald* should stand for a fair deal and public ownership, regardless of the capital that stood behind the concern. This was fair and just all the way round, and in fact was the best policy. Had the *Herald* and *Express*, known to be the property of the water magnates, urged some settlement unfair to the city or a renewal of the lease, it would have raised such a storm as to more than negative all our efforts, and would have been fatal to the papers besides. The *Herald* continued to be Democratic, as it had always been, and the *Express* was independent in politics, as before. There were no consultations between Charlie Willard and myself as to matters of policy, not even with respect to our attitude on the water question. But as soon as we were situated so that we could do so, our mechanical departments co-operated fully to accomplish what saving was possible. The columns of Associated Press dispatches, which we set at night, were transferred in the type to the forms of the *Express*, and, supplemented by the day dispatches, newly set, appeared in that paper. In turn, we took over the ready-set type of the day dispatches from the *Express*. It effected a considerable saving in composition, and gave both papers larger budgets than they could otherwise have had. There may have been some exchange of reprint and other reading, but if so it did not amount to much. Local news and editorial matter had to be entirely distinct and individual for each publication.

At that time Mr. Hellman was erecting his three-story brick block on the corner of Fort (now Broadway) and Third [Second] streets, and as soon as it was completed, we moved the plants and offices of both papers into it. The business office of the *Herald* was on the ground floor at the north end of the block, facing Fort Street, and the press-room for both papers was in the basement

[5]In the 1860's the city nearly gave to private owners a perpetual franchise for providing water. In 1868, except for one vote in the council, it would have sold the water plant and franchise to Dr. John S. Griffin, Prudent Beaudry, and Solomon Lazard for $10,000. Instead, the city offered a thirty-year contract (not fifty, as Spalding says above) to the same group for $1,500 a year, later reduced to $400. This was the contract which Spalding mentions as expiring in 1898.

beneath. The joint composition room and the separate editorial rooms of both papers were on the second floor. The business office of the *Express* was in the same block, but on Third [Second] Street, facing south. It was a very convenient arrangement for co-operative management mechanically, but kept separate and distinct fronts for business with the public.

I had drifted by gradual stages into [both] the business and editorial management of the *Herald*, while on the *Express* there were two men engaged, and the two tasks were segregated. I should have insisted on a similar arrangement on the *Herald*, as the double burden was too much for one man to handle. But I was accustomed to packing heavy loads, and thought I could get away with this one. The outcome was that I put in ordinary hours in the business office, and then worked until about midnight in the editorial room. At first I took the burden of filling the editorial columns, but gradually came to a system whereby two outside men furnished a part of the matter, for which I paid them space rates. Gen. Lionel Sheldon and Carlyle C. Davis, seasoned newspaper men, were glad to earn modest compensation in that way, and their contributions eased the pressure on me.[6] Still I had to inspect and pass upon all the articles, and I read proof on them as well.

I set out with the ambition to make the *Herald* a decent paper, and held to that standard throughout my administration. It was idealistic, but perhaps not practical. Our reporters had instructions to get all the news, and present it in as terse and straightforward a manner as possible. In those days none of the papers reveled in the details of crime and feasted on scandal as the sensational press does now. In our editorial columns we did not indulge in the cheap, blackguarding cross-fire with our "esteemed contemporaries," which was more in vogue then than now. We had positive opinions on every public question, and we set them forth as vigorously as we could, without descending to personal abuse or vituperation. We tried to be truthful and fair in all our utterances, and if we fell into error, were willing to make correction and apologize.

I still retained my small holding of stock in the *Times*, and for fear that, in conducting an opposition newspaper, some compli-

---

[6]Lionel A. Sheldon had been one of Hubert H. Bancroft's staff in southern California in the 1880's. He is listed as a journalist in the city directories of 1896 and 1897 but does not appear thereafter.

Carlyle C. Davis is in the city directory of 1898 as an editorial writer on the *Herald*, but he is not reported in other directories from 1896 to 1901.

cation might arise, I placed my *Times* stock in the custody of Col. Otis, and gave him power of attorney. Throughout my administration I maintained pleasant personal relations with the members of the *Times* staff, as well as with all the other newspaper men in the city with whom I had contacts.

We went through a presidential campaign, and strongly supported Bryan and free silver. I thoroughly believed in the cause, and have never recanted. The men who stood for restoring silver as a basic money metal were not the radicals, the visionaries, the semi-idiots they were painted, but they were the real conservatives. They were holding for a standard which had been maintained by the civilized nations of the world, time out of mind. This standard had been partially broken down by the Congress of 1893 at the dictation of the money power, and before the question had been adequately discussed by the people. In other words, Congress took snap judgment on the country. There is where the radical, the revolutionary action lay. Bryan, with his silver doctrine, was not a progressive, but a reactionary. He sought to recall a condition which had been abrogated by the government several years previously. Reforms never move backward. We cannot retrace the trail of lost opportunity. Hence, Bryan and his cause were doomed to defeat. Great Britain, when she felt herself the established money center of the world and sure that no other nation could ever challenge her position, led in the demonetization of silver. France followed; then other European powers. The money changers of the United States thought that we must follow suit to prevent all the others from dumping their silver upon us, withdrawing all our gold, and leaving us on a silver basis alone. Now see what the whirligig of half a century has brought about: Great Britain has lost her commanding position as the money center of the world. With her stock of gold as the sole basis of her currency greatly diminished and flowing rapidly away, she was obliged to discontinue gold redemption, and go it alone on her national credit. Had she held to the double standard from the beginning, her solid metal base would have been sufficient to tide her over the crisis. In an over-confident mood she tried to stand on one foot, and that foot finally failed, and she was down. Already there has been talk among English statesmen of restoring silver as a money metal, and such action would not only strengthen British finance generally, but it would be a godsend to impoverished India. If such a thing should happen, it will be amusing to see some of those people who have passed all these years ridiculing and reviling the "silver fanatics," eat their leeks.

In local affairs, the water question, upon which the *Herald* was in a ticklish position, was finally settled on the report of the board of arbitration by the city paying two millions of dollars. It was probably a high price, but it was a profitable investment for the city. I got through the ordeal without taking partizan ground for the water company, and there was no complaint or remonstrance from our backers. But there were other matters that troubled me more. Los Angeles had been laboring through hard times for several years [ca. 1893-1897]. I have already noted the temporary closing of the First National Bank in the acute stage of the crisis. But with that institution rehabilitated, and hopeless insolvencies adjusted, people were turning their eyes towards better times, which they flattered themselves were lurking around the corner. All we required was a good rainy year, to break the long dry spell, and we were ready to launch upon another boom. The fall and early winter promised well, but the season altogether was a bitter disappointment. Providence did not temper the wind to the shorn lamb. So far as I have been able to observe, it never does. There is no beneficent Providence that looks after the welfare of sheep or men.

The business of the *Herald* and the *Express* had shown some improvement as the result of the new spirit which we had thrown into them, the fuller dispatches and the better tone generally, and our mutual economies were working to our advantage; but all this was lost in the slump of another dry year which the community had to face. The summer following was harder than hard. In the fall we revived our courage and were ready and hopeful for another start, but the same exasperating disappointment followed. And the third year it was no better. We were simply laboring through a cycle of dry years. At this stage, a crushing blow fell upon me. Our oldest son, Hamilton, a fine, handsome, intellectual boy just coming twenty, was taken down with appendicitis. We called our family physician, who after prescribing palliatives that were of no avail said there was no alternative but an operation. We hurried him to a hospital, and the operation was performed before noon, but the surgeon pronounced it a serious case, with complications, and did not give much hope. Ten days later the complications developed into peritonitis, and the surgeon as a desperate resort decided on another operation. The boy was placed on the operating table, but died before the anaesthetic could be given. This blow was my finish. In my overstrained condition from overwork and the disappointment of long deferred hopes, I was in no condition physically or mentally to meet such an ordeal. I decided that, if I continued longer under the strain, it would finish things for me in short order.

I had a debt at the Los Angeles National Bank of $2,000, for which my *Herald* stock was pledged. I notified my associates that, if they would pay the debt, they could have my stock. I satisfied Mr. Kinney's claim of $10,000 by turning over real estate that he was willing to accept. I deeded him the Downey Avenue place, our Temple Street home and a valuable lot on Toberman Street. In the boom times that came later, those properties might have been sold for $25,000 or more. But I got out of the muddle without bankruptcy, which I greatly feared. While my drastic action might appear emotional and panicky, subsequent developments showed that it was probably the best thing to do.[7]

The owners of the *Herald* carried along for a year or so at a loss, and then sold the concern to a man named Hardison, who had made a fortune in oil at Ventura. Hardison ran the paper several years, blowing in his fortune, and considerable sums for his friends.[8] Then Tom Gibbon, a friend of mine and a keen attorney, took the paper and labored with it a number of years.[9]

[7]"One might think that, if I had shown more hope and confidence, more stick-to-itiveness, I might have weathered the storm and carried through to success. This question I have asked myself ten thousand times. But in viewing the situation in retrospect, and in the light of subsequent events, I have always returned to the conclusion that my course was for the best." From one of the late chapters, not used in this edition, of Spalding's "Autobiography," Groff copy. It is interesting that, except for the implications of his earlier mention of free silver, Spalding does not refer to the reason for resignation which he gave in his final editorial, *Herald*, Jan. 10, 1900: "My resignation is not the result of any personal friction or unkindliness with the management, but simply because there is something of a divergence in our views on public questions. Proprietorship confers the first right of control. I hold views concerning issues prominently before the country which the stockholders of The Herald regard as too extreme and too radical for even a Democratic paper to take.

"With the facts before me and such capacity for reading the signs of the times as I possess, I cannot believe otherwise, and I must say what I think."

[8]In the city directories of 1899 and 1900/01 Wallace L. Hardison appears as president of the Columbia Oil Company, the Eastern Star Oil Company, and the Los Angeles Oil Exchange. From 1900 to 1904 he was president and general manager of the *Herald*, with Richard H. Hay Chapman as managing editor. Chapman had been working for the *Herald* since at least 1896 and in that year was also involved as a publisher of the weekly *Spectator*.

[9]Thomas Edward Gibbon was an Arkansan who studied law in Little Rock, served in the Arkansas legislature in 1884, came to California in 1888, bought the *Herald* in 1907, and sold it in 1911. In one of the final chapters of the "Autobiography," Groff copy, Spalding described Gibbon as "a shrewd and successful lawyer, who had been a member of our [the *Herald*'s] board of directors and our legal adviser. He had financial backing of which the public was not advised—I have always suspected that it was *Times* money. But even he failed to command success, although he carried on a good, high-toned paper."

He finally sold to William Randolph Hearst who took the Associated Press franchise for his *Examiner*, and converted the *Herald* into an evening paper. He made the *Herald* yellow, of course, and that must have been what the public wanted, for the hoodoo was thus broken, and the paper started on a career which has brought great success. In fact, so great was its rebound that it has finally absorbed its principal competitor, the *Express*. Thus history repeats itself in a sense, for our water company investors combined the two in a provisional way. But they did not go far enough. They failed to make the papers yellow.

INDEX

Abbott, William, 23
Adolphus Perkins, 49n, 82n
Aguirre, Martin, 123
Ahn Goon, 135
Alden Fruit Drier, 68-71, 112n
Aliso Street tract, 60, 80, 110
Alles, Fred Lind, 141
Allison, Mr. (newspaperman), 41n, 42
Allison, Berry & Co., 41n
Anaheim, 68
Antelope Valley, 118n, 140n
Arcade Depot, 123
Arcadia Hotel, 31n
Arroyo Seco, 50, 58, 122
Associated Press, 128, 142, 147
Aunt Ann. *See* Hamilton, Ann
"Aunt Polly." *See* Pearson, Dana C.
Aunt Winnie, 87
Ayers, James J., xiv, 15n, 18, 36, 38n,
  89-90, 91, 98-100, 103, 114-115, 131n,
  140n
Azusa, 76, 78, 79-80

Backman, "Mam," 25, 27
Baker, Milo S., 98
Baker, Robert S., 31n
Baker Iron Works, 98
Balboa, 109
Baldwin, Elias J. ("Lucky"), 78, 84,
  116
Baldwin, John M., 34-35
Baldwin, Leon McL., 34
Baldwin and Beane, 34n
Ballona Lagoon, 109
Bancroft, Hubert H., 143n
Banning, Phineas, 13, 22n, 51n, 52n,
  53n
Banning, William, 53n
Bassett, James M., 28-29, 30, 32-34,
  101n
Bay, Elizabeth, 85
Beaudry, Prudent, 18, 21, 26, 30n, 59-
  60, 63-64, 87, 91, 96-97, 110-111, 142n
Beaudry, Victor, 96, 97n
Beaudry and Belshaw mine, 22
Bell, Alexander, 111n
Bell, J. A., 48
Belshaw, Mortimer, 97n
Berry, F. E., 41n, 42
Billings, Josh, 76
Bixley, M. J., 18

Board of Freeholders, xvii
Board of Public Works, 34n
Booth, Newton, 100n
Boyce, Henry H., 120, 123-125, 127-
  128, 129, 130n
Boyle, Andrew A., 111
Boyle Heights, 111, 123
Bradbury, John, 140n
Bradbury Block, 140
Brady, James, 50-51
Breed, Levi Newton, 127
Briggs, Mrs., 86
Brook, Harry Ellington, 133
Brooklyn Heights, 111
Bryan, William Jennings, 144
Budd, James H., 139
Building and Loan Commission, xi, 138,
  139, 141
Bullard Block, 19
Burdick, Horace, 20
Burlingame, A. H., 85
Burns, Robert, xviii
Burton, George W., 133
Burton School, 133n
Byram and Co., 120

Cajon Ditch, 44n
California Building and Loan
  Commission, xi, 138, 139, 141
California Construction Company, xviii
California Fruit Growers Exchange,
  xvi, 138n
California Institute of Technology, 128n
California Railroad Commission, 99,
  115
California State Printing Office, 115
California Truck Company, 28
Capitol store, 101n
Carmany (J. H.) and Co., 27n
Carmelite Sisters, 138n
Carpenter, Francis J., 45, 128
Carrillo, Pedro, 49
Carter, Nathaniel C., 116
Caystile, Thomas, 37n, 120
Celis, Eulogio de, 21n, 36
Celis, Pastor de, 36
Cemetery, 112-114
Centennial celebration (1876), 6n
Centinela Ranch, 31
Central Pacific Railroad, 3, 52n

[149]

University of California, Los Angeles, 97*n*
University of Southern California, 58*n*

Valdez, Julian, 21*n*
Vasquez, Tiburcio, 22, 57-59
Vejar, Pedro, 21
Verelo, Miguel, 18*n*

Waldron, Mr. (of City Council), 113
Warner, Juan, 49
Water company. *See* Los Angeles City Water Company
Waterman, A. F., 47
Water supply, 26, 31-32, 63-64, 96, 97, 145
Weekly Mirror. See Mirror (Los Angeles)
Weiss, A., 105, 106
"When Grant's the Ruler of Our Land," xix
White, Stephen Mallory, xiii, 102, 140*n*
Whitehead, Charles, 103*n*
Whittier, John Greenleaf, 42
Widney, Joseph P., 58, 64
Widney, Robert Maclay, 24, 27, 58*n*, 102
Widney, Sam, 24
Wilder, John, 103*n*

Willard, Charles Dwight, 133*n*, 141, 142
Wills, William Le Moyne, 44
Wilmington, 13, 21, 22*n*, 51
Wilmington Transportation Company, 52, 53*n*
Wilshire, H. Gaylord, xvii
Wilson, Benjamin D., 59*n*
Wilson, Percy, 136
Wine making, 54-55, 59, 61
Wise, Kenneth D., 57
Wood, Dr. Enos Parker, 8, 13
Wood, Fred W., xiii, xvi, xvii, 8-15, 25, 26, 44, 70, 81, 84, 87, 96, 103*n*, 114, 135*n*, 140, 141
Wood, Leona (Pigné-Dupuytren), 135*n*
Woodcuts, 92-95
Woodhead & Gay, 97
Workingmen's Party, 98, 99, 102*n*
Workman, William Henry, 21*n*, 66, 111, 113
Wright, Edward T., xiii, 44

Yarnell, George, 18*n*
Yarnell, Jesse, 18*n*, 37, 39-40, 72, 118-119, 120
Yarnell & Caystile, 37
Yarnell, Caystile & Mathes, 118
Yarnell, Caystile, Mathes & Otis, 119, 120

MAP OF
THE CENTRAL PART OF
LOS ANGELES
1885
ADAPTED FROM
STOLL & THAYER MAP
OF THE SAME YEAR

RIVER

STREET

ROAD
RAMIREZ
HOWARD
CENTER
ST
ST
ST
STREET

OLD MISSION
ST
KELLER

VAIN
STREET
STREET
FRONT ST
LOS
ANGELES

UN
ST
LAZARD
ST
ST
STREET
ST

LANE
WEILL
ST

ST
LAFAYETTE ST
AMELIA
ST

STREET
VIGNES
CENTER
STREET

STREET
MACY

HEWITT ST
GAREY

1. Plaza Church
2. Sisters of Charity School
3. Former Site of So. Pacific Station
4. Pico House
5. Former Merced Theater Building
6. Farmers & Merchants Bank
7. First National Bank
8. Good Templars' Hall

9. Temple Block, also known as Newmark Block (Express Office here 1871 to 1876)
10. Court House
11. Times - Mirror Co. (in Downey Block)
12. Former Site of Star Office
13. Herald Office (in Jones Block)
14. Old Jail
15. Nadeau Block
16. Turnverein (Turner) Hall
17. Fort Hill Cemetery
18. Former Site of St. Athanasius Church
19. Future Site of Times Bldg. (after 1887
20. Future Site of Hellman Block (Herald and Express Offices after 1898)
21. Future Site of Bradbury Block (Herald Office here ca. 1894 to 1898)